Thunder Overhead

By
Charles R. Millhuff

Thunder Overhead

How a little boy survived Chicago

By
Charles R. Millhuff

Leathers Publishing
4500 College Blvd.
Leawood, KS 66211

FOREWORD

The floor had the smell of oiled wood. It was old and worn and burnished with time. Sunlight poured over it through the huge double-hung windows with sills heavily varnished and deeply cracked. It had the air of forever and was furnished with things like hardwood, iron and slate. Everything was bolted down and always in rows. The place had as much individuality as a piece of chalk. Such was this pile of brick and stone I remember as Chicago's Eberhart Grade School. Three stories high with a six-foot iron fence around its gravel play ground, it was not unlike a prison.

The greater prison was in my young mind, not unlike the space beneath the lid of the desk where I sat. My tools of learning were stored beneath the lid of my own desk, which was bolted to the old oiled floor on the opposite wall from the windows. Good boys sat by the windows. My wall was the one with the clock near the door with the transom. The transom was cracked in May to let in a breath of air. This room was called the home room. To associate this room with home seemed a little bit strange. Still does. Here we learned of sounds or phonics and notes and dark lines. Lines we were to color within and write along and stand in.

The memories are mostly not good of this childhood. The tragedy is that, by and large, the teachers were much like the place, a fortress called school. It was not until decades later that my child's mind broke loose in a man's head. Like the lid of that desk, it finally was ripped clean off its hinges. Healing has taken place, but that's another story. What might have been? I ask it again and again. What might have been? I ponder as I walk in memory's dim light through the neighborhood of my childhood. The tall school halls with milk-colored globes, glowing at the end of chains hung from high ceilings. Porcelain drinking fountains in these halls are fitted with five chrome spouts. Like a pig's trough, they are bolted to the walls and above them the sign NO SPITTING. What should you do with it? Swallow it? Of course! This was the theme of the place, "swallow it." And so I did. But shall I still?

It really is the horrid fear of rejection that drives us from the risk of challenging the past. It's much easier to swallow it. Walk up to it, and with both hands open the lid. Who or what could still be in there? If monsters, aren't they now surely old? If memories, might it be that you have lived in mis-conception? If moments, wouldn't it be good to live them once again if only in the twilight of yesterday's opaque remembrances? Be a child with me again. Fill your hands with the garments of those young days. They are few at best when compared to the whole of your life. Stride into the future clothed in the best of the past. Why cheat your spirit of the spiritual? Press your heart against a living thing. A THING THAT WAS AND THEREBY IS. Go ahead into the place of your living — kick the back door down! It may shed the light you've needed to find the front door to the rest of your life. After all, you are the accumulation of all you have been. How can you love yourself if you don't know who you were? We are not "you" or "me" or "them"; we are all a collection of it all. They are still there. They wait to serve you. Monsters, memories and moments. Go ahead and stop. Turn around. The best is not always just ahead. Sometimes you have to give it time to catch up with you. Some things take a long time to be born. Let them!

Under that desk lid so much has changed. So much of it for the good. It is mixed in with the matrix of the good and bad, born of the years. Walk ahead with me into the past of my life, into the south side of one of the world's largest cities where once a very little boy lived in the early 1940s. And he lives still. There was more under that lid than I could ever have dreamed. And it is good … now! Those brick city streets talked. I just wrote a lot of it down. I was a child again. I found that a lot of me still is — though that child is old and worn and burnished with time.

The Viaduct at 65th and Central Park

Chapter One
THE VIADUCT

THE VIADUCT

WE LIVED two houses from the B & O Railroad tracks. They went over the little street our house was on, creating what we in Chicago called a viaduct. It was two tracks wide with room to spare, and when we heard a train coming — it could be both heard and felt — we would run and wave to the engineer, pleading with him to blow the huge, huffy whistle and throw us chalk. They used the chalk to write on the sides of the box cars to designate railroad information. We used the chalk to lay out hop scotch on the sidewalk. I loved that viaduct. It was cooler in the suffocating summer under there, created great pools of water in a storm and was a wonderful place to build a snow fort during the winter, protected as it was from the sun.

These are my earliest memories of Chicago where I was born and raised. This was the house I came home to from the hospital. To me it was never a home; it was always a house. It was built of brick, a part of the post-Chicago fire building code. It had no personality. Personality is a matter of comparison. There was no comparison. They were all the same. Block after block of them: little two-bedroom, shotgun houses with alleys behind them and gangways between them. They were no more than five feet apart. All had coal chutes and flower-box holders built of concrete set in the brick front wall under the two front windows. The door was on the side, a third of the way down the gangway. The backyard was a tiny plot. My life was simple. We played on the street and in the school yard. After school I waited for my dad to come home from the factory. Often I walked with my mother behind her green shopping cart to and from the A&P. And, of course, we went to church.

My childhood was lived under that viaduct listening to those huge trains thunder overhead, wondering in my little mind if I would ever make thunder of my own. Well, I did, and this is the beginning of that story. These are my memories now fifty years later. I've been back there, and much of it remains the same: the manhole covers, Eberhart Grade School and its cast iron fence and fortress-like building, the fire hydrants and the little streets where the leaves were burned in the fall before we knew that everything in the world was killing us.

I'll bet they learn someday that cancer comes from catsup. I can still hear my stern-faced dad say as I bumped some out on a thin slab of Spam, "Charles, why do you put that stuff on everything you eat?" Who knows! Why do dogs smell the end of a dog the way they do? They do it all over the

4

world. I've seen them in Africa, the Pacific, Europe and, of course, at first on the south side of Chicago. I used a lot of catsup. Dogs smell the last thing I would want to smell! Wonder why my dad never asked about the dogs? Maybe he knew. It's the kind of thing he would know. He knew about a lot of things. Not in an arrogant way; he just knew. What he didn't know much about was little boys. Often I would think about that under the viaduct, sitting on the curb playing with a little steel dump truck in the accumulated dirt next to it. It was a small residential street without much traffic, so I was, for the most part, undisturbed.

That is not to say that we never had disturbances. Those dogs I referred to would, on occasion, copulate in public. They would become connected end to end and would make Miss Schmidt very disgusted. She would pour water from huge old pails on the poor things, but to no avail. She, one time, let loose a powerful blast from the garden hose which emitted a laser beam of water from the brass nozzle at the offending dogs. Believe me, a connection of the canine sort brought me out of the viaduct. Miss Schmidt wasn't married. I think it made her mad to see intimacy at any level. I know that now, but then I really had no idea what was connected. I hadn't been to school yet, and folk didn't talk about those things in the early forties. They talked about THE WAR.

Three Years Old

Chapter Two
EARLY WORDS

EARLY WORDS

I CAN DISTINCTLY REMEMBER trying to talk when it seemed I didn't know any words. In spite of this, I know that I comprehended the concept of conversation. I remember saying a word that stopped the whole table. It wasn't a bad word; it was just a real word. And I remember it had syllables. I had made the sounds, phonetic sounds that adults recognized. I had spoken. Communication had taken place though very one-sided. I might have been two years of age. It was at the dining room table. I was in a wooden high chair. I had connected, yet I know not how, or what, or to whom. It was a phenomenal experience. A wonderful remembrance. Whatever was that word? How I wish I could recall it. But then it was not what I had said, it was what I had done. I, of course, can't even defend the idea that I know that they knew, I just do. It was my first remembered verbal connection, though at the time void of cognitive reality, in the interpretive sense. I knew I had connected verbally but didn't realize how. Mind you, I was about two with virtually no sentence structure ability. But the fascination of the event has yet to leave me now these fifty-plus years later. I remember the room. The window across from where I sat looking out on the yard. The crack in the plaster ceiling. Oh, yes, it happened.

Communication has become the heart of my life. Oral communication is my stock and trade. It has been the business of my entire adult occupation.

More and more words were to leak through and start to collect in pools or categories: nouns, verbs, adjectives and subjects. They just evolved. Grammar was learned by hearing and eventual constant correction. I learned how to talk. How to talk! How to verbally communicate. It was a wonder. I do remember the marvel of it.

Then came the crushing blow. No one seemed to care what I had to say with my limited vocabulary and infantile subject matter. So I learned early on to talk to myself. Often only within my head. My best friend was my brain. Often I would go to the railroad viaduct two houses from our home. As the thunder exploded overhead and as a long line of coal cars rumbled past, pulled by the great steaming iron horse, I would go beyond the cerebral interplay and voice my oration at the top of my lungs. Shouting with all the pipes of my squeaky little voice, I would tell the world my story. It was not until years later that my voice deepened into what it is today, but this was a greater issue than tone placement and the projection of sound. This was verbal self-actualization. It may have been the first time as a person I gained existence in the adult world. I had gained perspective, making sounds that connected with others of the species.

Children were to be seen but not heard. How stupid. Tulips are to bud, but not bloom? The horn is to blast steam, but not emit tone and sound? The train was to pass, but not thunder? What a mixed-up conundrum for a three-, four- or five-year-old. Little children need to be listened to **very carefully.** Not so much for what they are saying but for what they are doing. I mean, for heaven's sake, I talk to my black schnauzer dog who growls and yips and gurgles in response. Her little acorn brain is in a full-fledged effort to connect. So was I.

It was more than a cute or stupid juvenile noise. It was my soul attempting a connection with my surroundings. The effort continued on into school with interruptions in the classroom, with blurted-out, unwanted and, for the most part, illogical additions. Again, not what I was saying, but what I was doing.

No wonder I have been driven to become an articulate word smith, honing the fine art of the pause, developing painfully plain diction and the fluctuations of volume and tempo. The drilling eyes. The playing of the podium like a prop. The near maniacal drive for logic that leads the mind of the listener down a primrose path of gut-wrenching reality gilding out often onto a deep lake of gleaming stillness and understanding.

I speak well because early on I wasn't heard. I wasn't heard. The dynamics were not understood. It seemed no one cared to know what crashed about in a little boy's head. The thunder over my head is now in my heart. And, believe me, at times it roars, followed by painfully long periods of silence that I milk from the receding thunder of quietness. I learned how to be heard. Not only for what I said but for what I am and for some poor benighted souls for who I am, which is usury of the worst sort.

My cathedral, a viaduct. My audience, the rumbling trains. How long ago, but so real and close to this day. It's not being listened to, it's being heard. That was and is the issue.

The voice of one crying in the wilderness. I mean crying tears of pain in the shadows of the oversights. These were early on experiences. Long before I went to school. No wonder I exploded when I got there. I needed a padded cell or a parted heart that would allow the entrance of a little boy's verbal run at "being." The trains heard it, and on occasion answered, with the great steam whistle or the clarion engine bell. And, oh, what a response they gave. The trains didn't understand the words, great dumb iron things that they were, but they responded. Or, so I believed. A train is a great thing to believe in. Its thunder is always the same. From first word to last, it's there to listen. The thunder always listened. I wish the others had as well.

Third Base

Chapter Three
GAMES

GAMES

MY **DAD** called it a cardboard table. Not a card table where cards are played, because our religious niche didn't play cards. (We snuck around with Old Maid, and later in college, I learned to play Rook.) In spite of these limitations, I remember the games we played in the early '40s on the south side of Chicago. Games are important. They create the possibility of winning over and over again no matter how often you lose. They teach strategy and manageable tragedy as well as compassion for the vanquished.

Games, at their best, were created with cans, ropes, pennies, manhole covers, curbs, walls, hiding places, crab apples, sidewalks and chalk, balls of all sorts, snow, your own hands and feet and, of course, your brain. We also used string and hoses and sprinklers and tablecloths as tents over what else — tables. Well, that's enough. You get the idea.

Kick the can still clatters in my ears. I've kicked a Campbell's soup can all the way home from school and back, time and again. I've stomped on two cans, one on each shoe, and clumped around like a monster. We've played tug of war, swung from trees, tied each other to trees or lamp posts, and tripped many running souls with the same rope stretched across the darkened walk of the viaduct and pulled up to the one-foot level with perfect timing. I've lagged pennies at a line on the sidewalk or against the school building wall, gaining or losing capital on the eventual proximity of the coin to the line or building. Manhole covers were used for all sorts of games — home plate, for instance, or the point of the two goal lines for another. A crab apple flung from the end of a long, whippy, thin branch is a fearful thing to say the least. Hopscotch on the sidewalk was played with the outlines drawn from the chalk thrown to us from the guy in the engine or caboose. The possibilities for snow were endless — forts, snowmen, snowballs, snow angels, snow caves, sliding and just plain rolling around in the stuff. There were footballs, baseballs, basketballs, tennis balls, golf balls, to name a few. Life to a child depended a lot upon games. No television yet. We had to "go out," and as someone put it, get the "stink off us."

The games of the neighborhood had meaningful and lasting value inherent in them. We learned about winning and losing, being picked or not picked on a side, elation and embarrassment, and lessons in survival and evasion. Creativity was important as rules were altered to compensate for, say, no right field. There was the creation of brand-new games with everyday objects. (Tires, culvert pipes, coal shovels as sleds to be pulled or ridden, stilts made from clothes poles and my favorite, the scooter. A 2x4 board about 4 feet in length with half a roller skate nailed to the bottom on each end and a peach crate nailed to the front top end). Hours, I mean hours, I rode these things I made.

Of course, the great enemy of it all was rain. I had to stay in. No television. The radio forgot children during the daytime. And sitting under the kitchen table with a blanket over its top pretending we were in a tent fighting the Germans had its limitations. On one of those rainy days, I took a ball of string and unrolled it, tying it from lamp to lamp all through the parlor and into the kitchen where my sister sat bored. I told her to give the string a good pull, which the dummy did. She broke one end-table lamp, a floor-lamp globe and dented three shades. She pulled the string, but I got the beating. Wow, I can still feel the sting of that one, and the remorse, as my mom cried over her damaged beautiful treasures. It was so dumb to do, but it seemed to me a game. My dear sister deserved better but, at that age, putting one over on your sister was the grandest game.

"Mother, 'May I,' Simon says." "You may take one giant step or two baby steps or even a scissor step." Red light, green light in the fading twilight. Oh, how the memories dance like the fireflies that we collected in those mason jars on stifling hot

Chicago evenings, with the smell of the world's largest stockyards fouling the air in momentary wisps.

As I reflect, however, I know in my deepest and youngest heart that games were more than play things, they were pain things. The worst was not losing but rather not being chosen. The real sting came at the high school level when out of some 200 boys you made every cut until the last 12 were chosen, and then your name was not on the list hung in the gymnasium vestibule behind the glass of the bulletin board. It's a real part of life, and I might add, a necessary part. Early on, a general philosophy must be reached by the "powers that be" between winning and participation. Virtually all schools vie for winning, and they should. The real world does.

But at five, six or seven years of age, losing is a bitter memory. Not because it is wrong or unjust, but because it hurts. To play hide and seek and have no one come to find you just plain hurts. To play "Mother, May I" and for Simon to never let you, or to be the last chosen for a ball team, or to use the hand-over-hand-on-the-bat method to determine the last one to play, again, hurts. I'd hold the knob of the bat handle, my fingers like a chicken's claws, only to have it kicked so hard it sailed out of my hand, banging haphazardly on the asphalt street announcing my exclusion. This was at the very philosophical heart of competition's cruelness. It toughens you for good or for bad. I hated not making the team. Not being in the circle. Not being, yet so wanting to be, one of the ball players. The same ones over and over who made those childhood teams were the ones who eventually got real school uniforms and lockers with names on them at the high school gym.

Games are not games, they are life. I worked it out on my own. I didn't know who to talk to as a child. It's not only the fear of the contest, it's the acceptance that goes with it. In fact, that's the heart of the matter, and it all starts so early. Being little and shy and not gifted was the challenge. The games were everywhere. In the neighborhood, at the Sunday School picnic, even in kindergarten (kick ball, tag in the school yard, crack the whip, dodge-'em, etc.), games made their point.

I, again, identified with the trains. They always won. They were literally the kings of the hill. Those moments of gamesmanship in my early memory made me what I am today. I did not end up on a railroad siding, with a line of cars going nowhere. The streets of a great city are filled with reality for a little boy. They are a classroom of truth. Games may have taught the most.

And now, late at night, on a driveway under a moonlit Kansas sky, you can sometimes hear the bouncing of a basketball and see a man in his mid-fifties pulling up for a ten-footer. Occasionally, it hits the back of the net just over the front of the steel orange rim. Sometimes the chords rip as it glides through. It's not Kansas, it's Chicago. He's not in his 50s, he's real little, straining with every effort not to shoot but to throw a ball bigger than his chest at a hoop with no net.

It wasn't a game then; it's not a game now. It never will be, and that's a shame. Only the trains win. They're bigger. That part of the thunder is definitely still in my head, but the ball is also still in my hands. Thump, thump, thump. It's Kansas, but it's not.

Bolted down

Chapter Four
HEAVEN

HEAVEN

Sitting Under the Viaduct as a five-year-old, I was never alone. If you would have driven by in your pre-war Pontiac, you would have noticed but one little boy playing at the curb or leaning against the concrete on the inside wall of the underside of the bridge. There I would sit in the coolness of that interesting place. Again, you would only see one child, but there were two. When people say that a child plays well alone, they really are misunderstanding what is actually going on. I always talked and played with that yet smaller child within.

It was the real me. The one that no one talked to or noticed. My only real friend was that other little me. When asked, "What are you mumbling about?" I was talking to my inner self. I was asking the questions that big people were not aware of or, for some reason, avoided.

When I was spanked, which was often, my naked bottom was connecting with wires right to my inner heart. The unfairness so often left rage in the person you could see and touch as that person did his best to protect that little inner child. The reason I loved the viaduct with its massive amounts of concrete, forming arches and railings and straight side walls, was because it seemed so safe under there.

Its safety was proven over and over as thousands of tons of great steam engines and coal cars and loaded box cars thundered overhead. The trains were there. I could hear them, feel them and smell them, but they could not get to me. The viaduct, that wonderful viaduct, covered me and protected me: I mean both of the "me's." We were safe or, at least, had the illusion of safety.

I can still feel my arms wrapped around my knees with my heels tight against my seat, sitting there watching the occasional cars go by. When they rolled over the great cast iron manhole cover, it would rattle or, more accurately, rumble in a cast-iron sort of way. De-dump, de-dump it would go as front then back wheels rolled over it. Chicago, to me, was not the loop, or State Street, or Michigan Avenue or the Outer Drive. At five years of age it was a manhole cover, a viaduct, builder's marks on sidewalks and fire hydrants. My world was very small. The geography of my soul was very limited. But it was enough. It was a big place for me.

My dad had a unique way of calling us home from near or far. He put his two index fingers in his mouth in a "V" shape and created the most ear-splitting whistle ever heard. That meant to come home right then. I know now that you whistle for dogs, not people. I know I'm being unreasonable here, for we weren't on the farm where a bell could be rung, but that whistle — it still sends chills through my stomach, not up my spine, and it's been 50 years ago or more. More often it meant dinner or time to come in for the night. Kids being "out" was accepted then. Dogs and kids ran free. The boundaries were, by and large, our own fears of getting too far from home.

It was clear that about this time something began to happen inside me that truly frightened me. I know it started before I went to school, so I must have been at least four or younger. My inner self would begin to enlarge or, to put it better, it would amplify. The outside "me" with skin would observe the inside me. More than observe, it would experience, yet in a detached way. As if radio signals were being sent from that guy in there to me. Sounds, any sounds, became louder and louder. That rumbling manhole cover would sound like an explosion. Movement would increase to blinding speed. The cars would fly by like rockets. Colors were so vivid and increasing in intensity that I thought my mind would burst. After a while, I knew that if that inner me went far enough with this, I would never come back from wherever this was taking me. I remember trembling when, finally, the phenomena would start to subside and finally die.

I never told anyone about these spells, ever.

They occurred, as I remember, about once a month or so and seemed to have no connection with anything I understood. It did not stop until well into my second year of marriage at the age of 23. I had the last one in Indianapolis in Dean and Joanne Spencer's apartment and not one since, although I've felt a very slight twinge of it a few times since then but not within the passt ten years.

What was going on in the other me? Who was that person called the "inner child" by so many who study and write about these things? Why was there no one to tell this to? What in heaven's name was going on? It was frightening to be so un-integrated, so to speak. Was it the trains? Was it my aloneness in a family of five? Was it the fire and damnation I heard at church literally in the womb and beyond? Or was it the real me screaming for some help or love in the midst of a cold, hard city? I have no desire to go to Chicago now. I often fly into O'Hare Airport and feel a sense of great unease. I read Annie Dillard's love affair with Pittsburgh and Thoreau's miracle moments at a pond, but not so with me in Chicago.

The only thing I loved was that viaduct, and I know I never had a spell under there that I couldn't fight and win. Protection. It's a funny thing, isn't it? Fear is, I believe, not genetic. You learn it. Slipping out of reality at four years of age makes one wonder, though I have no remembrances of overt abuse (a fact I have confirmed with my older sister). The temptation is to construct a regression crisis. Some regression is real and releasing, but much of it is constructed to explain inappropriate adult behavior, thereby dissipating responsibility.

I have so little to go on at 56. Some old photographs, a visit to these places that I made with my wife and children a few years ago, and my memories. Memories of a red dump truck and a curb and a viaduct and the thunder over my head. What I can go on is that there are still two me's, and I have learned to take care of the little one. I have found viaducts in my present world. They are not so much places I go to, but people I can be with in spirit and, more importantly, in truth. They know who they are. My son, my daughter and my wife of 35 years. There are others, fewer than five, who are there.

A viaduct. Viaducts. Everybody needs them. And they are not God. I mean God is not the viaduct. If anything, God builds them. He built one for both of us; who I was and who I am or am becoming. Two houses down from the tracks in the misty memories of my childhood mind is where the first me began. I have never been a "me." I have always been an "us." And therein is the real drama of life. The stuff Shakespeare wrote so well about. The elusive truth that Hemingway and Faulkner searched for and today Annie Dillard chases and writes about.

Someday I'm going to go back to that viaduct

and sit there again. The passing folks will think I'm among the homeless. In some ways, I am as are we all. It is then we understand, to some degree, our own personal immortality. Is it heaven? If so, it may be shaped like a viaduct. I rather suspect it is.

My School

Chapter Five
EBERHART GRADE SCHOOL
CHICAGO PUBLIC SCHOOL SYSTEM

EBERHART GRADE SCHOOL
CHICAGO PUBLIC SCHOOL SYSTEM

THE PAPER HAD WOOD in it. I don't mean in the overall sense that most paper has wood pulp as its primary ingredient. I mean this stuff had chunks of wood in it that pencils had to traverse. It was during the war and good smooth paper was hard to get. My second grade teacher used it to draw on with pencils, charcoal or colored chalk. She held a bunch of it cradled in her arms in a stack and drew on it. It seemed like magic to me because it was upside down to her as she faced the class. I can still feel the texture of that rough paper and smell the scent of trees.

There were so many things to experience at Eberhart Grade School through the senses of a seven-year-old. They created the matrix of sensations that were the background for a young human experience. Chalk dust in the air. The smooth desk top with the clinking ink well lid made of cast iron snapping shut over the glass ink well liner.

I still — even in my mid-50s — flip those little lids on restaurant creamers, satisfying a primal remembrance. They're ink well lids with the wells set in the oak desk top, bolted to cast iron pedestals, anchored to the foundations of the earth. Again, **clink, clink, clink**. I sit in restaurants and level and twist the lids until they are as they were in Eberhart Grade School.

And then there was the feel of the rippled, wrinkled varnish on the window sills of the huge double-hung windows. They held deep cracks, the results of 50 summers of maintenance doing battle with the blistering Chicago sun that poured through the great panes of glass.

The varnished floors, how they gleamed. One morning they stopped their gleaming when Billy Wisener, whose father owned the bakery on 63rd Street, lost his breakfast during the pledge of allegiance. The pungent smell of vomit brought tears to 25 little sets of eyes as 25 little stomachs wretched.

Our custodian was an old, large woman with a great pail fit with a wringer and a grand mop of immense weight and size. She leaned over to remove the foul-smelling mess. Some of the mop she directed with her foot. She bent over, revealing the knots of her nylons bundled behind each knee. She smelled of old cleaning things. She first used red sawdust to soak up the worst of the mess before she started to swing and then toe the mop touching up the last of the puke. I can still see her swinging the thing like a great flood of righteousness across the fouled area. Great messes were horrible but soon cured. When you are young, things are catastrophic and blissful all within a moment or two.

As I remember, there was a lot of going to the bathroom and vomiting in the second grade. The vomiting was spontaneous but not the going to the bathroom. We lined up for that just as we lined up for almost everything. The boys and girls stood, often twisting and turning in anguish, at opposite ends of the hall. We lined up and marched into our bathrooms single file. The great urinals were built for 20-foot-high men, and the stalls were separated by great slabs of granite hung with paneled oak doors attached with chrome-plated hardware. Boxes hung high on the wall, filled with water, for the great flush. These were fitted with pull chains ending with porcelain knobs. Once pulled, the great load of water came crashing into the flushing process. Thus the familiar and famous poem and melody:

> **Pepsi Cola hits the spot,**
> **even though you're on the pot!**
> **Push the button, pull the chain,**
> **there goes Pepsi down the drain!**

O, the poetry of my youth; a sideline in this yarn. Stays with me long years after those limericks of spelling have faded — to say nothing of Keats, Tennyson and Longfellow, which were to come in later years. All this real literature ground into the gravel of the playground, surrounded by the penitentiary iron fence, and blown off onto the wind during play. I well remember **Pepsi, Pepsi** and **There Was a Young Man,** and much of what Confucius was reported to have said.

So much lining up in those days. We lined up for the drinking fountain, lunch break — which lasted an hour and was eaten at home — milk time, recess, trips to the library, to say nothing of my solo trips to the principal's office. (Strange title, prince of pals.) But, back to the bathroom. I knew a kid who could pee all the way over those back-to-back urinals in second grade. The show created a delay that brought the teacher storming in just in time to see the glorious golden rainbow.

The gymnasium was on the third floor and had a cork floor. Climbing ladders were bolted to the walls. Leather-covered monkey rings hung from the rafters. Tumbling mats were on the floor and, of course, basketball goals were ten feet off the floor. Painted stripes of black and red were all over the floor in circles and lines, most often used to stand at or around for order and, at times, even for the playing of a game.

Remember this was during the war and all of us were getting fit for our crippled leader, President Roosevelt, for whom we collected dimes to defeat the great disease of Infantile Paralysis, or as we came to know it, Polio. He was a victim of the same illness, ruling this great republic for 12 years from a wheel chair. **And we did it** ... with the help of a man named **Dr. Salk** and the March of Dimes, for which we filled up little cards until we had a dollar to proudly give to our teacher and the cause. We also sold garden seeds from the **Burpee Seed Company** for victory gardens. Our goal was to "Beat the Krauts and the Nips," names I am now ashamed of. War breeds prejudice cloaked in patriotism in the very young. Getting fit, selling seeds, collecting dimes and stamping on tin cans in the kitchen for bullets was all a part of supporting the cause.

The war all seemed to start in earnest in this gym where the windows were covered with cages. They were huge and let the sunlight drench this wonderful room in the afternoons. Sound in this place echoed as if in a dungeon. I loved it in there. Think of it — seven years old getting fit for war. Long years before televised sports or an awareness of sports radio, I knew that in that room was a place of great opportunity. Not only a place to help win the war, but a place to be something and, more importantly, someone.

Once the gym teacher had me step out of the line and announced to the class that I looked like a basketball player because of my long arms. That night I went home in a cloud of glory. With a black ink pen I drew a crude number seven on my underwear shirt. A uniform. **Mine!** It was my first and last uniform. Many things interfered with the dream. I can feel that silly-looking shirt with its self-proclaimed official number on my little back even now these years later. You had to have a number to count, so I made one based on that teacher's pronouncement which might as well have been given to the *Chicago Daily News*. The dream drained but that was much later. This was second grade. Then it was kick ball and rope climbing and medicine balls and the freedom to run free without reprisal. I loved her and the place and the spirit and the concept of the room. Win the war, get fit, maybe get famous. What a place. All of life for some, should have a gymnasium in it somewhere. I'm one of them.

The three main halls of the school, one on each floor, were painted cement. Gray walls and deep maroon floors were illuminated by hanging globes that glowed in a milky sort of way. All the doors had transoms over them with tick-tocking clocks next to them. The blackboards were actually black and made of slate. When raised they revealed sunken coat rooms. They were contraptions of rope and lead weights and pulleys — devices of wonder to a seven-year-old. I could lift a slate board weighing hundreds of pounds with my two little hands. I still remember the empowerment I felt in doing it, and I did it often. Even during class. I was corrected and punished often for unscheduled board lifting. Once I brought the heavy thing down so hard that a rope inside the contraption broke, sending the lead weight crashing to the bottom of the cavity. This released other doors above, somehow creating near decapitations on an upper floor. Wow! Right to the prince of pals for that one! I was curious, not overtly disobedient. I know that now more than I know anything about those days when I was seven. I wanted to do and learn and try out my immediate world.

All the banisters of the school were perfect for sliding with great iron posts anchoring both ends of the railings along the stair wells. The rails themselves were wooden and gleamed in the sun that splashed across the stairway from the landing windows. Of course, this was high on the forbidden list. Might fly off the end, hit the great iron ball on the post and knock your little rear end off. Why did they care? They tried to beat them off anyway, with hickory yardsticks and rubber-tipped pointers.

School buildings have a life of their own, and Eberhart Grade School was no exception. All brick and stone. Three stories high with a basement where the little bottles of milk were kept covered with ice for milk time. Here also were the great furnace and boilers. For nine years this school was **The Place** of my life. From nine to three, five days a week, nine months of the year, this was the place of my emerging. It was stronger than I was. It would not dent or bend or care. It would outlast me and had obviously long preceded me. I only passed through it. I sense no loyalty for the place or the people of the place but for a few exceptions. The young gym teacher whose pretty face I can clearly see but whose name I've completely forgotten; Mrs. Leonard, after whom the auditorium is now named, who sent me a birthday card in seventh grade, and Mrs. Garvey, the music teacher, who said I could sing. Her favorite was "My Grandfather's Clock."

Gravel, iron, painted cement, porcelain, oak, slate and chalk dust, and the women who ran the place. I didn't belong there, but I did. My report cards made the same point. Horrid failure, near perfect attendance. The building was built for the building, not for me. I was to conform to it or be broken by it. Through the breaks it created in me with its system, learning was to be poured into my seven-year-old broken self. It didn't work. I hated it. I still do.

It's hard to separate places and persons. Most of my classmates did, I think. I wish I could have, too. Too much to get around, over and through. But it was during the war. My war as well. 1945. Like the paper, it was rough.

Eberhart Grade School

Chapter Six
THE ALPHABET

THE ALPHABET

THEY STRETCHED across the front of our classroom, above the picture rail and the black-board. It was first grade and there they were. The heart of the whole matter. Somehow, I knew that this was the seminal core of all learning. Get this right and the world would be yours. The border-line of heaven. The place where it all started or ended. I slipped into my little alphabetically as-signed seat, and with my chin propped up on the heels of my hands, I knew they were the hurdles of all hurdles. The carriages of light that would lead to pure gold. All 26 of them, the letters of the alphabet. These were the individual bricks that could build a bridge that could get you from here to there no matter where here or there might be. Instinctively I knew this. All 26 of them had a large version and a small version standing at its side like its first born child. The matrix of what was done with these works of art, I could tell soon, was not only fabulous but fathomless. Too fath-omless for me.

First, one had to learn them by a name and be able to draw them on demand in or out of order or individually at a moment's notice. They all, when pronounced, had sounds and even special and unusual sounds when combined. Now what had been a whopping 26 big and little letters had magnified to become complex sounds in an innumerable collection of bits and pieces. At some point, someone had tipped over a large bowl of multi-colored alphabet marbles and they had gone everywhere. Some of the other kids kept them all collected as if their brains were perfect Chinese checkerboards with little holes prepared to hold the whole business in perfect order. They just sailed through it. I can remember how I so wanted it to be that way with me. But it wasn't. I could draw them after a fashion and worked ever so hard to connect them. I knew that, with the trains, the engineers were the ones who made up the trains and pulled them through life, leaving a floating cloud of smoke drifting over the spellbound bystanders. The rest of us only watched the trains go by. I knew then that the world would belong to the people who owned those letters at the front of the room over the blackboard. It related to spelling and reading but, most importantly, to knowing. I didn't know what that meant then, but I did. I suspected that knowledge and power were one.

If I wait for a moment, after all these years, I can again feel that deep, inner critical weeping to do this well. To do school. To understand all the maps and books and posters and things the teacher pointed at with her rubber-tipped hickory pointer with the brass cup hook screwed into its end. I felt a gulf between myself and this landing place of privilege and pleasure. I just didn't have enough jump in me at six to clear the chasm. I tried so often but failed and crashed time and again, missing even a slight hand hold on the distant edge. My lack of success was often seen as a lack of desire. How wrong they were.

I could describe the room with all of its now old-fashioned style. The tick-tocking clock, the ink wells, the huge double-hung windows in Room 101, which was painted in gold leaf on the glass transom over the door. Even the alphabet, in green with the stuttering two red lines creating three levels through the letters from end to end and illustrating the proportion of each letter to the rest, was baffling. But that was not the issue. And I'm not sure we need to know the issue. At least, the issue at that level at Eberhart Grade School. The real issue was that the mind in the brain of a child was off the track with no one to reach down and simply set its wheels right. I plowed through the gravel while others sailed down the line. My story here is one of desire and stardust. Of a mind made of gossamer wings crumbling for some reason under the load of "th" or "ch" or "ba." Of then recoiling to the slight variations of "we" and "wi" and "wa." Adding periods and interpreting words made that chart at the front of the room become a million miles long.

A.E. Newton said "the buying of more books than one can peradventure read is nothing less than the soul reaching toward infinity." To roll up that strip of knowledge at the front of the room would at that point have been as impossible for me as had I tried to roll up State Street or the Outer Drive. Maybe I should have done grade one when I was nine. The trouble was I wasn't nine — I was six, and I had one shot at it. Then to cursive and paragraphs and comprehension until in my mind it was a blur.

When I walked into that room and cradled my chin in my hands that day and looked up at that highway to heaven, I never dreamed it would become my walkway to hell. But it was. With the sun streaming in through those huge windows in Room 101, playing across the oiled oak floor, casting rows and rows of desk shadows across the hardwood floor lines, my soul soared at the idea of learning how to learn. Learning how to learn. What a wonderful idea. One must never take it for granted. From a little desk to the letters at the front of the room high on the wall may be a steeper climb than Sir Edward Hillary's repeated and finally successful assault on Everest. It was for me.

Teachers *are* human

Chapter Seven
ON THE TOILET WITH
CAROL KEARNEY

ON THE TOILET WITH CAROL KEARNEY

I **DON'T KNOW** if it's a matter of folks not listening or my inability to speak clearly. It is a fact, that in my adult life, I have made a commitment to speak clearly with good diction and, most of all, with legitimate authority.

As a small child, I was not heard. This has been the fountainhead of my adult quest for a hearing or someone to listen to me on the smaller scale of one-on-one and recognition on the larger scale of national notoriety. I have become a very good public speaker, or so I have been told. It was not always so.

Speaking out in class was by far my most grievous sin in those first years. It was not what I was saying but that I was speaking. I did not want answers to my questions; I wanted interest in my personhood.

In third grade Mrs. Simmons tried to teach us the style and beauty of cursive writing. We learned the Palmer Method — endless spinning circles and connected rows of up and down strokes, line after line, page after page, using a straight-nibbed ink pen.

Mrs. Simmons had a clever sign next to the

old tick-tocking clock up on the wall next to the transom over the door. It read **"Time will pass — will you?"** Well, as a matter of fact, in third grade, I didn't. I remained in third grade to try it all over again. And try I did. I'm sure at the end of the year I knew no more, but the teacher did and wanted no more of it.

I did not want to perfect the art of penmanship. I wanted to write something to Mrs. Simmons. I wanted to be heard. I was a little boy less than five pounds at birth — four pounds, eight ounces.

There was one person who heard me. Either the man in the red caboose at the end of the train or the engineer at the front. I would stand on the street below the train and yell with all my might, **"Chalk! Chalk!"** And occasionally one of them would throw me a piece of huge round chalk used to mark box cars for routing, etc. Yellow or white, what a wonderful gift! Under the viaduct or on the sidewalk I wrote large words that no one could miss: "I'm Charles." Then I waited for the train or others to see it. It was great! I could see what I said marked in big yellow or white letters on the sidewalk. I felt good about that. I still do.

Carol Kearney also heard me. She was a special friend in third grade. She was my secret friend. When I was sent to the hall for punishment, she would often ask to be excused to go to the bathroom so we could talk. Once when I had been banished to the hall, I saw the dreaded principal,

Mrs. Smith, heading my way. I was terrified at the prospect of her finding me there. Carol suddenly appeared and saw the whole thing developing in a moment. She led me into the girls' bathroom, which was adjacent to our third grade room. "Quick, Charles," she whispered, "in here. Stand up here." Into one of the stalls she rushed me and told me to stand on the seat between the granite dividers with the oak paneled door closed and locked.

She sat on the front of the stool with her legs showing beneath the door and her Oxford shoes barely touching the floor.

Mrs. Smith never missed a thing and was into that washroom in a flash. Her "hello" was greeted by Carol's, "Hello, this is Carol Kearney."

"Just checking," the principal remarked as she left the room.

What an escape! My heart was pounding like a big base drum. Carol peeked out the main door, watched her disappear into her office and told me the coast was clear. I let go of the great stand pipe that was attached to the bottom of the oak flush box.

Carol Kearney didn't only hide me, she heard me. She heard me when most of the rest did not. What a trick we pulled. Soon I was back in the hall sitting on the floor next to the door, and she was back in the room. I was seven and I'll never forget it.

To be heard is a wonderful thing. The man in the caboose, Carol Kearney. It's hard to remember the others who listened. People looked at me, talked at me, ordered me, or just ignored me.

Carol was different. There were limits to what she could do when I flunked third grade. My twin brother, along with Carol, moved on to fourth grade. She was helpless to help me there, but I know she would have if she could.

I love you, Carol Kearney, wherever you are. It was a high point in my early life ... literally. To be heard, in reality, is to be loved.

Chapter Eight
IT'S ENOUGH TO MAKE YOU SCRATCH YOUR HEAD

IT'S ENOUGH TO MAKE YOU
SCRATCH YOUR HEAD

THE IDEA OF THESE THINGS coming right out of your brain was a little unnerving. It all started with a new twist on a first grade school day. We were all asked to go to the gym on the third floor. Single file. No talking. Walk by the wall. Six-year-olds trying as best they could to not behave like six-year-olds. Up the steps to the first landing, then the next and the next to the third floor, where we waited in line, of course. When we had all filled our space along the wall, I was in near proximity to the gymnasium doors.

Suddenly, they burst open and out filed a whole separate class. Most of them scratching their heads and offering to us their impressions of what we had to look forward to. Comments like "weird," "Did you see that thing glow?" and "Maybe they cooked my brains" were a few of the remarks.

We filed in after they all left, and were marched to a waiting line that ended at a table with some medical people directing the operational procedures on what appeared to be the fate of the whole school. I didn't have a ghost of an idea what it was all about. No one seemed to be in any pain and it was a change, a diversion, so I was gobbling up the whole scene. When the line had inched along far enough, it was obvious they were examining our heads. Well, now this was making sense to my young powers of reason. Checking for brains. Now the showdown! Weed out the numb skulls or, at least, the empty ones.

There I saw the device up close. A floodlight bulb on a gooseneck lamp stand. I'd seen one in the doctor's office when I slipped off the step ladder, hit my chin on the top step and nearly bit my tongue in two. Blood everywhere. My mom came running when she heard my screaming and saw me, an oral fountain of blood. She grabbed a tea towel, jammed it into my mouth and we headed for the doctor on foot. Well, that's another story, but there in his office I saw that kind of a gooseneck lamp contraption. The bulb emitted a fluorescent purple glow and a smell I distinctly remember to this day.

"Next," I heard, and with trepidation I stood next to the table as the great glowing goose looked down on top of my little melon-sized cranium. "Yep! There's one, and there's another," they said. "Stand over there." Well, I thought, they found something, so I must have brains in there. Geronimo! I'm one of the geniuses!

Wrong! The kid next to me shared the pleasant news, "Guess what?"

"What?" I replied.

"You've got worms." So who's going fishing?

Again, I did not have a ghost of an idea of what he meant. I soon found out, as the school nurse took us to the far end of the gym over by the monkey bars to learn the medical truth. We had ring worms on our heads. I couldn't comprehend it. All I could imagine at six years of age were worms crawling out of my brains taking a "look, see" through my hair at the larger world. Holy Moses! What a revolting development. Believe me, you haven't heard the half of it yet. Our folks were called for immediate pick-up. We learned that these babies would jump from head to head. Maybe they should have been called spring worms. Very contagious. So I walked home with my brother and sister, who had the same affliction having been sprung upon or having sprung, we'll never know for sure. The doctor was called and instructions given.

When my dad got home, the first of the procedures began. In turn, we stood in the bath tub as Dad used the old, dull hand clippers to shave, cut and primarily uproot every hair from our little skulls. I can still feel the itchy hair on my shoulders, tumbling down my back to the tub and me yelping with every snip, rip and clip. When it was done, I was shorn, torn, worn and in total confusion. Where were the worms? In my feet now? After all, I was standing in a cut pile of their abode. After all three of us went through all the screaming and "please stand stills" and "just a little mores" and "it's the doctor's first order" and "you can't go to school unless," it was over. My dad sat on the stool with the lid down, of course, totally pooped. Pardon the pun. Mom cleaned up the hair and gathered up the little curly suckers in a bag of hair to burn in the furnace. Ring worm smoke for the whole neighborhood! Here it came, ready or not! Get a good sniff, it'll give me a little satisfaction as you make jest of our head gear in the days to come.

We were at the doctor's bright and early the next morning to be examined by an identical goose-necked lamp glowing purple and emitting that strange smell. Might have been the little worms frying on the grill of my skull. It's too grim to look up the facts. Our heads were painted with a foul smelling discoloring potion, and we were told to keep them tightly covered. "Tightly" was explained to my mom. "Tightly" was installed at home. These caps were made from discarded women's hose — placed low on the forehead, so as to cover the entire area of hair growth. They were twisted on top like a modern trash bag and then again pulled down tight over the face. This gave the appearance of a pervert or a bank robber until the overlap could be trimmed just above the eyebrows. All diligence was used so as not to sever an ear or put out one or both eyes.

Yes, even in 1944 we had a sense of style at the grade school level. Boys wore high-top boots with hook-and-eye laces, complete with a pocket knife pouch. Girls rolled their bobby socks down just above their shoes. I knew of no such luxuries but I was, at six, aware of the feelings of "same" and "different." "Same" was good and "different" was not. The point of this is that these perfect fitting **"chapeaus"** were in the extreme "different" category. So, off to school we went to join the "order of the ring" that was, to some degree, in every class. How I wished Mrs. Smith could have had one of those little beauties take a run and spring into her bonnet. I'd have given my left arm to have seen our principal with one of her nylon stockings pulled down over her head, clicking her way down the hall in all her glory. No such justice. Soon the novelty wore off and the ridicule subsided.

But the stuff hung on. Trip after trip to the doctor revealed that we had a very severe case of this dread ring worm. The cure was not working. We sat under lamps at home, applied medications and wore the disinfected nylon stocking caps.

And then a truly remarkable thing happened. Our pastor, Dr. L.A. Reed, pastor of one of the largest and most historical Nazarene churches in the world — Chicago First Church of the Nazarene — came to visit us. His very presence in our home was unforgettable. Believe me, this to me was an "up there," "down here" perspective from every remembrance. This man, I know now, was a pulpiteer of the pulpiteers and considered a prince of a preacher and a presence in any room he graced. This great church pastor had, during the days of World War II and rationed gas, come a long way to visit three children with their heads in nylon stocking caps made of discarded ladies' hose covering a disgusting, non-life-threatening disease. It's like God had knocked on our front door to scratch a child's mosquito bite. I'm still impressed all these years later. I was afraid of him, but in those days I feared almost everyone. He sat down on our piano bench with his back to the piano and asked the three of us to come to him and stand in a line before him. He told us he loved us and knew our problem must be real embarrassing. He understood. He cut through it all. He had a small bottle of oil with him, about the size of your little finger, with a little black plastic cap that screwed off. One by one, he wet his finger with the oil, then laid it on our forehead, and prayed that God would heal our ring worm, calling us each by name. He prayed as if God knew who each of us was, and cared. Well, that was it. He exchanged farewells with my folks. I had no idea what had happened. If there was an explanation, I don't remember it. I know now he was following Biblical procedures outlined in the Biblical book of James as they related to all illness and disease.

Well, we all marched off to the doctor the next day to be scoped by the purple worm finder on what was a regularly scheduled weekly update on rings and worms and other pleasant items. One after another, we pulled off our footware lids and stood beneath the telltale purplish glow with the mysterious odor. One after another, we were asked to repeat the procedure as the doctor picked and rubbed and scratched around on our heads. He looked at my mom and said, "It's all gone."

She said, "What do you mean?" obviously forgetting Dr. Reed's visit the night before.

He said, "Mrs. Millhuff, I can't find a single worm on any of these children. They've just all disappeared."

We were told the hats were done, the painting was done, the shaving was done. We were well. The plagues of Egypt were driven right off our heads by our own Moses, Dr. Reed. The doctor cleared us with the school. I had been healed. At six, I was told it was a miracle.

Of course, I don't talk about it now. For heaven's sakes, it wasn't melanoma or a brain tumor, it was ring worm of the scalp. But I will tell you this, most people don't get over the little critters overnight, but we did! And I believe God healed me. It happened in our living room, in front of a piano bench where Dr. Reed sat. Unbeknownst to me, it was my first direct connection with an omnipotent, all-powerful God. Dr. Reed, six years old, ring worm, healed, God. It's a train I didn't connect for years to come, but when I finally did I could still hear the distant thunder far over my head. The rattle of a miracle in the mind of a child. Many have been the times I've scratched my head and thought about it. God was at work in my life as a child through others. I was not aware of it in a little house on the south side of Chicago a long time ago. Was it Dr. Reed or was it God? Or both? It is enough to make you scratch your head.

The Principal's Office Bench

Chapter Nine
TILL MY FEET TOUCHED
THE FLOOR

TILL MY FEET TOUCHED THE FLOOR

THE FIRST DAY I went to school is one I will never forget. I can feel its sharpness in my left arm even now. I'll explain that later. Of course, I had often been to the school yard, walking through the dungeon-like wrought iron gates swung wide open and each chained to the equally heavy fence. The whole play yard was pea gravel — not a blade of grass anywhere. The fortress-like brick and stone and the great front staircase leading to the great front doors made of very heavy wooden timbers were imposing. I'd looked in there a few times but this was the day to go in.

All the paper work had been filled out. I was enrolled. I was sent to school. I walked with my sister, who hated every step of the way. When I was a kid, your mom didn't take you. In Chicago you just got to the day that you went to school and you went. I was five. I was dressed in dark blue corduroy with a tan shirt that had a collar whose points lay over the straps of my overall pants buttoned to the overall bib that covered my chest. I was quite the sight. My oxford shoes were scuffed. They were only shined on Saturday night for church. The Lord's day had been rough on my shoes and so they were as they were. And so was I as I was. In a word, very hyper! I was frightened and extremely energized all at the same time. Conflicting, ambivalent emotions were among my most painful young memories. I was off to kindergarten.

I was met at the door by some big shot and directed to the kindergarten room. It was the first room on the right after you climbed the stairs to the first floor. I actually had envisioned a garden in there. Probably a victory garden. Remember it was 1943 and the war was on and we all planted gardens of Burpee seeds.

The door was open and the sunlight was pouring across the varnished birch floor. On the floor was painted a large red circle right in the middle. As the other children arrived, my hyperactivity rose accordingly. There was no place to hide here. No skirts to shrink behind. No viaduct to retreat to with its cool dark safeness. We had each brought a hook rug. These were, we learned, to sleep on. Sleep, you say! When nap time came, I was so high my rug could have flown. I tried to lie down, but it was impossible for me. It was probably about 11 o'clock. I had earlier spotted a sandbox in the corner. I left my bed and headed for this play place. It never dawned on me to ask permission. I just got up, stepping over these little souls all laid out on their little hook rugs, some, in fact most of them, dead to the world. Can you in your wildest dreams imagine sleeping on the floor your very first day in school and only two hours into the event? I can't, and I didn't. I made it to the sandbox and stepped in, sitting on the corner. It was then that the teacher saw me. This was no fresh, young, just out-of-college teacher. This was a real Chicago battleship! The faculty of these hundreds of Chicago schools were like a fleet of them. I never remember a young teacher in all my grade school or high school days with the exception of my gym teacher. The battleship asked me what I thought I was doing. I didn't have to think; I knew what I was doing. I was sitting in the sandbox playing in the sand. She pronounced the name "Charles" like it was the start of the apocalypse. The little rug rats shot up rubbing their sleepy eyes like a gun blast had gone off.

"Charles, will you come here!"

I was frozen in fear and embarrassed with 40 little eyes in 20 little heads staring at me in the corner sandbox. I didn't move. I couldn't move. I can hear her chair scraping the floor as she pushed back from her desk, both huge hands pressing against its edge. She started toward me, then towered over me. She had a handkerchief in her hand that she stored up her sleeve. Why would you put a handkerchief there? But she did. When she was about five feet from me, my only thought was protection. I grabbed the only thing I had — sand. I threw it at her. Over and over I threw sand at her until she retreated straight out the door leaving it wide open. I remember the transom, the ticking clock next to it and the blackboard along the whole wall washed clean for the new year. It's all frozen in time for me now. A sandbox to sit in when you couldn't sleep seemed the most normal thing in the world to me. Not in Room 103. I even remember the number on the door.

She returned with reinforcements. It was the principal, Mrs. Smith. She now reminds me of Margaret Thatcher, the past Prime Minister of England. This woman was formidable. She took in the scene in a moment and walked straight to me without hesitation. She wore a dark blue suit with a white blouse and had big shoes with thick heels that pounded the birch floor as she closed in on me. She reached down with her bright red-nailed fingers and lifted me bodily out of the sandbox by my left arm. I couldn't keep up with her as we headed for the door, and I stumbled. But I had no need for fear of falling; her grip held firm. So firm, in fact, I can still feel her sharp red nails embedded in my left arm. Down the hall to her office where I was planted on a long pew-like bench in the outer office. Secretaries peered over the counter at this five-year-old, his feet swinging in rhythm to his pounding heart. What she did, I now realize, was call my mother who, in turn, called my father who, in turn, left the factory and drove to the school to get me. And get me he did!

Mrs. Smith used the arm; he used the ear. We

passed 103 on the way out. How I wanted to be in there. How I longed to be normal. We got home in a flash and to the basement we proceeded. He went about the job of fixing me with a peach crate slat — a familiar routine: pull down your pants till you were bare, over the leg and then bloody murder, a lecture, reminders of the marvels of my sister who preceded me in school with a perfect record, and then the deal about this hurts me worse than it hurts you. Huh! I never got that part too well. Of course, I cried. It hurt. The whole day hurt. As the afternoon wore on, I made my way under the viaduct to regroup my life. Soon the kids came home, and there I was. Well, it was my space so I closed my ears to their remarks.

My first day at school. What a start. Was I a bad boy? I know now I wasn't. Was I a dumb boy? Again, I now know I wasn't. For heaven's sake, I'm now a well known preacher of the Gospel with an earned doctoral degree. Why couldn't they see who I really was? How badly I wanted to be inside the red circle. I know now all of life has these red circles in the middle of its realities, and some folks are better at staying on the hook rug than others.

I went back; I did better to a point. I spent a lot of time with Mrs. Smith for those nine years. Finally, my feet touched the floor from that bench. But she never really touched me. Mrs. Smith. For some reason, I want to be like her. It's complex. Let's just leave it at that.

Chicago Sidewalk 1913

Chapter Ten
SIDEWALKS

SIDEWALKS

SIDEWALKS TO A CITY BOY are what country lanes are to one who grows up out there. Sidewalks have cracks about every four feet or so. These are put there by the one who lays the sidewalk in anticipation of the breaks that will occur as the temperature changes from blistering heat in summer to Arctic cold in the winter. Concrete is porous and contains water and expands and contracts, especially during freezing weather, making the inevitable cracks. There may be long intervals of unbroken sidewalk, but then there is the unevenness of a slab that has heaved up above the rest along one of these prepared cracks. The company that lays the sidewalk would typically imprint a seal in the wet cement to identify it as their work and when they did it. We called these fishes. Superstition runs deep in the city. We knew if you stepped on a crack you would break your mother's back. To step on a fish or the square that a fish was in was of even greater seriousness. Maybe your own back was literally on the line. People put footprints or handprints or initials or even obscenities in the wet concrete that lasted for years. For all I know, they're still there.

There were sidewalks and "gangways." These led from the sidewalk to the front door or into a gangway between the closely spaced houses. Sidewalks were clearly "public property." This point was plainly reiterated millions of times a year by children as they protested the eviction notice delivered by another child who in anger was breaking off a relationship with them and wanted them out of the whole neighborhood. Of course, the sidewalk, a scant 30 feet from every home's front door, was public property. Many a real fist fight had broken out over this dispute.

One day Billy Hubbard went into our backyard and stole a large stalk of my mother's rhubarb. I caught him in the act, which only served to provoke him into an attitude of rebellious ridicule and name calling. I, of course, evicted him from our property to the sidewalk. There he stood at the end of our gangway using language that would have brought my life to an end in the basement if my dad ever heard it from me. He kept one foot half on the sidewalk and half on our gangway. Part public, part private. The language and taunting continued. The rhubarb had long since been forgotten, though a rhubarb is exactly what we were engaged in. I have no idea why tough arguments are called rhubarbs, but they are.

Let me deviate for a moment to my mother's attitude about bad language. She would not even abide by what were known as by-words, words like heck, darn, gosh, golly, etc. These, of course, were substitutes for the real thing. Her punishment lingers yet in my mind, but more so in my mouth. We used red Lifebuoy soap in the bathtub, but Fels Naphtha in the basement for the wash. It was typically called "Brown Laundry Soap." With a bar of this vile stuff in one hand, Mom would hold my head in a hammer lock with the other. She would then proceed to wash my mouth out with soap, which meant rubbing, or more accurately, grinding the soap back and forth over my teeth until they were loaded. Then came the washing part which was totally my personal responsibility. It foamed and bubbled and was inevitably, to some degree, swallowed. I can taste it even as I write these words. I might also add that though my mother finished the associates diploma or the second year of high school, her grammar was perfect. She corrected us immediately when we erred, minus the soap. My grammar to this day is flawless, because I was taught to hear the right usage. Only years later was I to learn, to some degree, the mechanics of English, a rule-breaking language if there ever was one. Spelling was another story you've heard elsewhere. But back to Billy Hubbard.

Something in me finally burst and I rushed full speed toward Billy with my fists flying, intending to do some serious bodily damage on public property. He was taken aback and retreated at a dead run. I nailed him as he tripped on a treacherous

Our home like all the rest

crack in the sidewalk under the viaduct. When it was over, we were both bleeding and crying and exhausted, promising to bring our fathers into the fray as soon as they got home from work. Billy headed home, and I sat on the curb trying to sort out heavy issues as they pertain to public and private ownership and rights.

Sidewalks and gangways join. Sidewalks join gangways with their neighborhood homes and the people who live in them. Without expansion lines, sidewalks in between are impossible. That's where we meet most often. "You can't make me leave, this is public property" is yelled in executive board rooms, in private bedrooms, and even church rooms. It's the cracks you don't plan for. When they come, you both go down in anger, threats and pain.

It so hard to be too big to be little. It was then; it still is.

Desks like so much built on iron

Chapter Eleven
THINGS OF IRON

THINGS OF IRON

MANY THINGS IN THE CITY of Chicago are made of iron. I have learned that the same is true in the country as well. Iron things stand out in my mind — not steel. Steel was the girders that held up the elevated train that formed with its tracks a loop in downtown Chicago, giving rise to calling downtown "The Loop." The kitchen table was porcelain-covered steel. Cars were made of steel. This was steel. I'm speaking here of **iron.**

This brings up an interesting subject. Why was downtown downtown? Down from where? Of course, there was the north side of the city called the "North Side." Being south of the north side, one might call it downtown from that perspective. We lived on the "South Side." It was Sixty-fifth Street to be exact. Sixty-five blocks south from the center of downtown which was zero street. If downtown was downtown from the north side, then I **really** lived downtown at Sixty-third. There was the west side but no east side because the east side was Lake Michigan. Downtown should have been uptown to us. One of the little quandaries of life that really doesn't matter a hoot.

Back to the iron. There were many things of

iron: the many parts of the trains as well as many other parts of traindom — the platform and railing mounts, the connecting rods as long as flag poles that drove the hot, misty steaming pistons mounted behind the engine wheels — and the iron fence around Eberhart Grade School. The school was a fortress-like structure, surrounded by a fence six feet high and extremely heavy. The front railings up the vast stone steps were of iron. The steps inside the school were all of iron treads with iron lattice. Three floors of them on both ends of the building. The wooden-topped desks were bolted to heavy ornate iron bases, and the seats were on oval pedestals of iron as well. The handles on the huge windows were of cast iron as was the door hardware.

Then there were the iron manhole covers and the iron fire hydrants. How grand on those hottest days when the fire department would open a hydrant for us to stand in front of. I can still feel the blast of water that crashed into my little body and ran like torrents under my viaduct into the cast iron grates of the storm sewers.

To me, cities are cold, cast iron places. Others speak of the beauty of the city. I never saw it. Oh, I can make a case for the skyline or the Washington Monument on Michigan Avenue or the turn-of-the-century architecture of the buildings glowing in the burnished light of the late afternoon sun. But that's my adult view. At five it was an iron place. A hard place. An unbreakable place. It broke you. You didn't break it. I could list iron street cars and drinking fountains and fire escapes and bars over store windows along the alley and door stops anchored to the school room floor. The milk wagon hitch and lamp posts and the furnace in our basement. Things not made but cast. Iron things that could not and would not change. In my young mind they had been there from the foundation of the earth and were connected to the same. So cold in winter, so hot in summer. I never saw the beauty, only the weight and strength.

I often tugged at the iron grate under the viaduct when the smoking, puffing, rumbling iron thing thundered over my head. So unmovable. So unstoppable.

Little people need soft things in an iron world. I learned to meet, and to adjust to, and to fear, iron people. I learned to love soft people — some turned out to be iron, some did not. Cities are made of concrete and iron and stone with little patches of lawn. So little lawn, so much iron. It's as I remember it, and it shaped a lot of my life. My style. Myself. I must admit, I'm tough. I learned it somewhere. Was it the iron?

Iron Storm Sewer Grate

Chapter Twelve
SIXTY-THIRD STREET

SIXTY-THIRD STREET

SIXTY-THIRD STREET was only a few blocks away. It was where my mother went to shop. She never drove a car all 79 years of her life. She pulled a little green shopping cart made of steel mesh with two red wheels and a simple rod handle. This street of commerce was a world of immense proportions compared to our little side street three houses from the tracks. Here was the A&P store where all the food was purchased. I learned much later that A&P stood for the Atlantic and Pacific Tea Company. Here was the European continent and all of Asia right here on the south side of Chicago in our neighborhood and I had no idea of the magnitude of the place. I do remember the big red coffee-grinding machine where my mom ground a bag of 8 O'clock coffee. After setting big pointing dials and placing a red, yellow and black bag under the square shoot, she pulled a big lever that would start the monster.

I had a fear of machines. They all seemed to hurt things. They ground up beans or mercilessly flattened wet clothing between wringers or sliced off grass (or toes) with the spinning blades of the reel lawnmower. Combining benefits and pain was an early point of confusion for me. I see that now, and have, as a fact, formed a whole well-developed philosophy of life around these perplexing issues. Suffering is the foundation of joy but, at three or four years of age, my little mind could only gawk at these paradoxes. I often hid behind my mother, filling my hands with her dress when these machines went into action.

Of course, the grandest of them all was the street car. It was made of red wood and iron and guided on embedded steel tracks in the brick streets. It was connected above to a snapping power line by a trolley that brought the power from the wire to the "thing" itself. These tracks ran off into infinity both ways on Sixty-third Street. Sixty-third Street went to the *world* wherever, and more importantly, whatever that was.

I felt better about the horses that pulled the milk wagon or the garbage wagon in the street or alley. I can still see the garbage wagon horse eating my mother's hollyhocks as the smelly, fly-ridden garbage was dumped by the garbage man over the slanted side of his wagon. The horse often wore a hat with holes cut for its ears. I never wondered where these horses lived at night. I reason now, given the size of Chicago, there must have been thousands of them. I can see the leather feed bag strapped over its head, and the great head throwing itself in the air as the beast worked for the last kernels of grain to grind between its brown and yellow teeth. These weren't machines. These were horses. In 1940 the city and the farm were still on speaking terms. I never saw a farm until much later and distinctly remember seeing my first cow at the Museum of Science and Industry, downtown, in a dairy display. They were milking the poor thing with a machine. It seemed cruel. Four of 'em pinched up under there like they were giving the creature a jump start. I sat down on my little heels and looked up under this marvel. It's the first time I knew why there are four quarts in a gallon!

That reminds me of the milkman who came inside after rapping on the back screen door. Straight to the ice box he went, checking for butter, eggs, milk and cream. Wanzer milk. I can still see the sign on his wagon: "Wanzer on milk is like sterling on silver." The long-neck glass bottles were replaced by square quarts with round waxy hole plugs in the corner. So much was replaced. The ice box became a Kelvinator refrigerator, the furnace got a stoker and the car lost its running boards.

Eventually, Sixty-third Street got new, sleek, green, steel street cars. No jumping on the platform any more. The doors closed like giant accordions. No conductor. The motorman did it all: gave change, opened and closed the front and middoors and drove the thing. This wasn't a street car; this was a tin can. Sixty-third Street was never the same again. Soon, all the horses were gone. The hollyhocks were way out of control, and I learned that Sixty-third Street was a street — an avenue — not a state of being. But in my mind it still is the place you go to go everywhere. Everyone needs a Sixty-third Street — I did. I still do.

My twin, Howard, at the wheel

Chapter Thirteen
IT ALL CAME OUT IN THE WASH

IT ALL CAME OUT IN THE WASH

BY FAR THE MOST REMARKABLE piece of machinery in our home was the Kenmore washing machine. It was in the basement next to twin tubs made of a stone-like material almost black in color and used to rinse the clothes. The process on wash day was simple. First into the washing machine. Then through the wringer into the first tub. Then again through the wringer into the second tub, then into the wringer and dropped into the wicker basket on the cement floor. Next, up the cellar steps to the clothes lines to be attached to the same with wooden pins. Clothes poles were placed strategically to hold up the sagging lines. They were made of cedar, my dad told me. They were about six feet long and were notched at the top end to fit the ropes. Without permission and with scraps of 2x4 less than a foot long nailed a foot or so from the bottom to the sides of two of these 1x4 poles, I made the greatest set of stilts ever. I walked around on these things like King Kong. Soaring above all of my playmates, I clunked down the sidewalk in front of our house. Unfortunately, I fell and broke one of the poles in two and soon had my rear end broken into four!

On top of the wringer was a panic button that you slammed if ever you were unintentionally wringing an item like your sleeve or hair or hand. These two hard white rubber cylinders grinding, extracting soap and water was a fearful thing to watch. I must admit I never saw the panic button slapped, but I do well remember waiting for it to happen. Typically, my brother and I would sit and watch through the basement window that was open for the occasion all summer. We poked our heads in as far as we could to see the marvelous event take place.

Once my twin brother had gotten his entire head and shoulders into the window to watch the mighty wringers blow up a pillow case — always the high point — and finally, with a great whish, go on through, dropping into tub one or two or the basket. It seemed the most natural thing for me to do was to give his little seat a push, since he had so hogged the view. Let him really see the event. Experience the event. Become existentially involved with the essence of the event. He fell into tub one, cracking his four-year-old head on the tub edge, mingling his blood with the soapy water. The blood-curdling screaming could be heard all the way to the school yard five blocks away. I was gone like a flash to the viaduct to await the news of his passing o'er Jordan's soapy tide. Soon my mother, with wet apron framing her legs, pulled me from my fortress and put me in the bedroom where my brother lay with a wet pink towel over his little split-open head.

By mid-afternoon he was up and about with a Martian-like lump on his skull. Of course, I felt bad, but not as bad as I felt when my dad got home and administered justice in the same basement next to the now silent washing machine.

I want my brother to know that I'm sorry for what I did. It was not premeditated nor was it a crime of passion. It was an act of impulse. We are separated by nine minutes; fraternal twins. In all these years my brother, Howard, the older, has never done an unkind or disloyal thing to me. So you can see it pains me to remember this incident now some 50 years later. My brother laughs about it; his head healed just fine.

As I reflect on all of this, it seems to me things were cleaner back then. Oxydol soap, the hot sun streaming through the sheets and towels and clothes. Sometimes I helped Mom carry in a basket partially full of folded things. Just enough so I could lift it. With my face pressed into it all, it had the smell of sunshine. I can hear the clothes pins dropping into the clothes pin bag that slid along the line from one end to the next. When finished, Mom wound up the clothes line on a wooden contraption with handles on opposing sides as well as opposing ends. Then there they were. Two pipe clothes line stands set in concrete in the backyard with their hooks empty on their two head-high arms.

Once in a while, I still see a wash on the line. Typically in the country. It seems a better way to do it. A non-chemical approach to freshness. The old green porcelain Kenmore washer. The two tub wash sinks and the old poles linger in my memory. I've said nothing about ironing and darning and turning collars on worn shirts. Of button baskets and starch on the stove and a world without deodorant which drove, to a great degree, the whole process.

Wash day, which was typically Monday, was a red letter day of interest and activity to a little boy growing up in Chicago in the early '40s. It seems now that the yard was as big as a football field and that there were miles of rope and sheets blowing in the wind like the sails of a 64-gun frigate. But I know it was not so. So much of what we remember was not so. Therein is the disparity of wonder and truth, reality and rapture, the child and the man.

But the trains and locomotives, they were everything and more than I remembered. From our yard, you could see them and certainly hear them, being but three houses down the block. So my memory is filled with things that were and were not. Coordinating childhood and adulthood is like going through life's wringer. And like the clothes, you do it more than once. Somehow life's cycle works. You might say it all comes out in the wash.

Chapter Fourteen
BASEMENT REPAIRS

BASEMENT REPAIRS

MY DAD REPAIRED EVERYTHING. No one I knew called anyone else to fix anything. Sink goose necks, peeling linoleum, broken windows, dripping faucets, loose chair rungs, to say nothing of things that squeaked, rattled, gurgled or banged. In my pre-ten years (not pre-teen) I took it all in. I found the repair of things almost God-like.

My dad did things on schedules. He painted *a* storm window on *one* side each night through the summer and reversed the process in the winter with the screens. He laid the screened frame out on two saw horses, pulled up an old rung-back chair and started. He pried the tack strip up very carefully so as not to ever break or ever crack one. These nails were called brads, as opposed to tacks, that held the screen wire mesh to the frame to start with. After the screen wire was removed, the frame was painted usually on successive nights. The new screen wire was trimmed to near size with huge scissors called tin snips. The screen wire was tacked to the frame and the now-painted tack strip was nailed to the frame, over the heads of the tacks, with brads. The corners were carefully mitered so as to fit a perfect corner. I've seen my dad make a whole screen main frame, long years before main frames referred to electronics and computers.

My father's hands connected to his brain were wondrous things to watch. Screens and storm windows were child's play compared to pipe fitting and electrical wiring. He could do it all: draw a fine "back saw" through a miter box, or cut, strip, curl and screw down a copper wire to a screw embedded in a porcelain switch. Things like saw teeth and screw threads and bolts and nuts that matched fascinated me. He understood it all. I learned. I watched.

I often tried it when he was not there. That little basement workshop was a wonderland to me. I have, to this day, an affinity for these things. A few points need to be made here. Things were fixed in the basement. Things were thought through first, then the hands worked miracles. I can still see the very tools that belonged to his father from whom I got my name, Charles. They had first belonged to my great-grandfather Millhuff. The great rip saw and the gleaming set of chisels. The marvelous wood plane with its paper-thin blade peeping out of the smooth steel sole. To watch wood curl out of this tool brings vivid memories of the smell of pine and the perfect turns of veneer-thin wood that were within themselves marvels my little hands held with wonder. Wooden vice clamps and a real woodworker's work bench with square holes to hold the stops and secure the work. Then the wrenches, the screwdrivers, the bits, the braces, the oil cans that popped when pressed with your thumb. "Just a drop is all it takes." I can hear him now. Same attitude as with catsup. I can't remember it all. I was so young and there were so many tools so perfectly arranged in boxes and drawers and hung on the wall long before peg boards had been invented.

The main issue here was the mentality of "how" to fix things. It's the way he tried to fix or repair me. Always in the basement. Always with a thought-out rationale. Always with a board — left-over screen stock — always with my pants down — pulled down by me before him — then bent over one of his legs holding my legs in place with his other leg. The place to repair broken five- or six- or seven-year-olds. The basement. "When we get home, go right to the basement" preceded many a Sunday meal on the way home from church, or school or wherever. The damnable, wonderful basement.

The tools, the wood, it hurts to this day. I cried and cried. It was another one of those several places of peace and pain, wonder and wrong. The conundrums of life.

If we could have sat under the viaduct and talked it over just a few times, I think I'd have less thunder in my head to this day. This thunder is painful as I write this. Today it would be called abuse. It's all this Godly, spare-the-rod-and-spoil-the-child cleaver man knew to do, and it was the only place he knew to do it. You see, it's where he repaired things. To this day, I don't like basements, yet I love the memories of the tools.

And the trains. Someday they would take me away from it all. I counted on them. And they did.

Chapter Fifteen
THE RADIO

THE RADIO

OUR KITCHEN TABLE was made of porcelain. It was actually steel covered with porcelain. It was white with a blue stripe around the top edge and had a drop leaf on each end. You could get six people around it. There were five of us. There were chips on it that seemed to have always been there. It made a grand tent when covered with a blanket.

On that table was a Philco wooden cathedral-shaped radio. It played the constant religious messages of WMBI, the radio voice of the Moody Bible Institute started in the 1930s and founded by the Billy Graham of his day, Dwight L. Moody. It was here as well that we listened to *The Lone Ranger, Amos and Andy,* and the news. A man by the name of Gabriel Heater was often the announcer and reader of the news, and by the marvel of short wave radio we actually heard the war in the background as it was described by Edward R. Murrow. The voice sort of came and went in a bending sort of way as if you were putting your finger on a record as it turned on the record player, first slowing it down, then letting it run full speed again. There was a lot of crackling and popping. The bombs exploding were there and the dive bomb-ers could sure be heard zooming around Murrow from his roof-top vantage point.

I was born in 1938, and all I can ever remem-ber of the news was the war. That did not end until I was seven, in 1945. First in Germany and then in Japan. My war remembrances were many.

• Stamping on tin cans on the kitchen floor. "To make bullets" I was told. How could you kill people with Campbell tomato soup cans? I won-dered. At four, I didn't connect the metal with the manufacturing of the eventual product.

• Lights out drills when the whole neighbor-hood went black and we waited for only God knows what. Men in tin hats walked the streets with arm bands they got from President Roosevelt and made sure no porch light was left burning. My heart pounded as I slid down next to the up-right piano in the living room waiting for the bombs to come. Edward R. Murrow would tell us about it in his crackling voice from some roof top in down-town London. But the bombs never came. To some degree, the fear never left. Destruction from out of the sky where God lived was very confusing to me. The same radio that carried the salvation mes-sage of Jesus on WMBI also blurted out the war of destruction and terrible death. I can still hear his voice now more than 50 years later. "The sky is a glow of orange and red with bursts of bril-liance as the bombs explode. Smoke drifts as the wind off the channel pushes it along. Buildings are burning everywhere. How long can this city stand? Is Churchill alive? When will the invasion begin? I'd better move now, they're coming in closer and closer to my position."

• We saved rags, newspapers, and as I've already said, tin cans. Gas was rationed. Sugar was rationed. Life was rationed.

We were at war. I mean *we* were. Not just them over there; I was. At four and five years of age, my world was blowing apart and soon it would be on my street. I could only pray that my viaduct would stand up to the bombing. That radio on the porcelain table and its mixed messages! First a lovely quartet from the *Haven of Rest,* "On a hill far away stood an old rugged cross; the emblem of" … "We interrupt this broadcast for a bulletin from the front … Adolph Hitler, the Chancellor of Germany, has just made an announcement about his intentions to invade Poland." (pause) Then short wave ranting and screaming of the mad man as he addressed thousands and thousands in person and millions by the wonder of radio.

The world was in the hands of mad men! They all lived in that radio and coexisted with religion, *The Lone Ranger, Amos and Andy,* and all in our little kitchen. Sometimes I just sat and stared at it in silence. What joy and pain, fear and peace that it brought to my little heart. Often I went to the curb under the viaduct and waited for a train and pretended it was the bombs. Life was a lot of thunder overhead — thunder I couldn't begin to understand — and it was coming out of a little wooden box on our porcelain kitchen table. Europe in Chicago, Hitler in our kitchen and the *Haven of Rest* in between. You figure it out. I couldn't. I still can't.

Chapter Sixteen
CHUCKIE GUBAH

CHUCKIE GUBAH

THE THING ABOUT CHUCKIE GUBAH that one remembers even from earliest youth is that the Gubahs had an upright piano in the kitchen, a very little kitchen. The top of the thing was covered with stuff like you'd keep in a kitchen cabinet. I mean stuff was piled up there: Wheaties boxes, cans of Spam, bread and even toilet paper! Right there in the kitchen was a piano. They often sat and ate at it. As a rule they closed the big cover, but in spite of this the keys were stained and had all manner of food stuff in crumb form between them.

You know, I never heard them play that piano, and it never occurred to me to ask them why it was there. Their house was on the end of the block on the same side of the street we lived on. These were dirty people. I remember. Or maybe they were just different. It seems now that at four or five or seven years of age, dirty and different were about the same. I know I felt much better than them. They were the first people I felt truly superior to. The thought of my name, Charles, being twisted into Chuckie makes me sick to this day. I feared that derivative taking place. Some tried it through the years, but I killed it on the spot. The fact that the name Chuck stuck (pardon the rhyme) is a little unusual given this background.

Here was the concept of differences between families, people, kids and kitchens. I'm sure I experienced "different." I just never knew it carried with it the potential of better or less or judgment. Who had told me that putting a piano in the kitchen was a strange thing to do? I don't know, but I distinctly remember that someone had. Whenever I think of the Gubahs, I see that loaded-down piano. I never went into their front room. For all I know, they had a refrigerator in there!

Through the years, I've met a lot of Chuckie Gubahs — people who did things differently. And, far too often, I have attached moral or ethical meaning to them because of their obvious differences, never trying to know the who and the what and the why of the situation. The Gubahs were people I could have known. Too bad I only knew about them. I never got beyond the kitchen piano. What a shame it was. What a shame it is.

Chapter Seventeen
COAL MINER'S SON

COAL MINER'S SON

OUR HOME WAS HEATED with a coal-burning furnace that sent the rising hot air up through a maze of round heating pipes to registers that were in the oak floors of the rooms of our house. The furnace itself was a huge cast iron affair with a contraption of grates, air inlets, the aforementioned delivery system and the great door into which the coal was shoveled and a cinder door beneath it where the spent cinders were removed. It was the heart of the whole house and to a child a monstrous behemoth more remarkable than any other thing in the place. Its door, when opened, was a sight to remember with the fire well stoked for the evening's fight against a bitter cold Chicago night flying with freezing razor blades off Lake Michigan — Chicago, surely the windy city. Poor folks didn't have fireplaces for cozy warm memories, they had furnaces of unspeakable fury. With the damper open creating a roaring draft, Dad would open the door and shovel in the required load from the coal bin and there, before my eyes, was a literal definition of a real burning hell. Whenever I heard sermons as a child on the subject, and there were many, my mind was at "the door" with the deep flames of red and orange and yellow defining the subject clearly. To this day, I can feel the heat.

The coal came in a coal truck. Its load was dumped through a small trap door in the huge tailgate of the gigantic dump truck. Beneath the tilting bed, at the point of the trap door, was placed a wheelbarrow with an inflated rubber tire. When the wheelbarrow was heaping full, the coal man pushed up the long steel handle that closed the trap door and stopped the flow of coal. He then hoisted these two wheelbarrow handles and rolled the load to the coal chute, which was near ground level, and dumped the coal into the coal bin, a room adjacent to the furnace. Trip after trip he made until the purchased amount was delivered, one wheelbarrow at a time. The dropped pieces were swept up from the street and sidewalks, and soon the great truck with the wheelbarrow chained to its back rumbled off down the street to accommodate its next customer.

The whole process was a marvel to me. Morning and evening, Dad would shovel the blazing thing full after first shaking the great lever on the side that let the burned-out coal, in the form of cinders, fall to the lower chamber where they were shoveled into steel baskets to be taken to the alley for pickup by the garbage man. In snowy or icy conditions, the cinders were sprinkled on the sidewalk to avoid, as my dad put it, "exposing the public to the risk of a nasty fall on the ice." He liked phrasess like "nasty" and "peachy fine" and "that's of the first order." The whole contraption was a marvel and made excitement for a five-year-old before T.V. or stereophonic sound came to our house. My dad took a special delight in that furnace, and I'll tell you why.

He worked for the Goodman Manufacturing Company of Chicago. It designed and built underground mining equipment — electric-powered mules that pulled the coal cars from the mines to the elevators that lifted it to the surface. Their company's claim to fame was a continuous mining machine that created the oval tunnel of the mine as it bored through the soft coal, dumped it out on a conveyor belt behind it and then loaded it into the cars that were pulled by the mules to the elevator. These great revolutionary advances in deep-coal mining happened where my dad worked every day as a draftsman, then a tool designer and, finally, as the master mechanic of the whole place. These marvels worked deep in the earth of southern Illinois, Kentucky and West Virginia among other places. My dad's life had a wonderful cycle to it. He explained that to me when I was a little boy, sitting on the basement steps watching him shovel in the coal. He helped design the machine that cut the coal from the earth that was delivered by the trains that thundered over the viaduct a few doors down the street. This coal was loaded into dump trucks and delivered to our house where it was dumped into our basement, a wheelbarrow at a time, and then into our furnace to warm us through the bone-chilling nights.

My dad's work had meaning. He had an understandable part in a chain of survival for not only millions of people, but literally for himself and his family. He loved his work. He was proud of those yellow behemoths shipped in pieces by train to be assembled at the mine site. I grew up believing that work had meaning. My childhood toy truck was a preamble to a life of meaning and value that I never stopped striving for. What undefined lessons we learned as children. How simplified and connected things were in a city that could be self-contained for a man like my dad. The work he did all day warmed his family by night.

Howard Goodman had hired my dad. We heard that story often. I watched a man leave for a factory before daylight and come home as the sun was setting. Here was a proud man who felt value in his existence. Not plowing the earth beneath an azure sky or laying hands of skill on the sick or framing the policies of government in a position of power. He held no such professional posture. **No.** He worked in a factory, mining coal for his family. And I was a coal miner's son and didn't realize it. Nor did it occur to me that the very trains that thundered over my little head had a coal car, first thing, behind the engine for fueling their very movement. Even they were fired to make the steam that powered them with their incredible strength. I'm proud that in Chicago my dad found value in work. I learned it from him as did Solomon of old. To Solomon, the fruit of labor was man's greatest joy; all the rest was vanity. And so it was. It sure seemed that way to a coal miner's son.

The Principal's Office

Chapter Eighteen
DOOM'S DAY

DOOM'S DAY

THE END OF THE WORLD IN 1944 was an ever present thought in my young mind. It's not as though I never enjoyed a waking moment without the thundering fear of its immediacy upon me, but it was, in its own way, always there. We knew Chicago was a place the bombers were aimed if ever they could get here. The blackouts, turning the city into an inky blanket, brought a lot of fear into my child's heart. Wardens wearing helmets and arm bands tapped on the door with their flashlights if they saw the slightest twinkle beneath a window shade from within our house. We huddled behind these shaded and draped windows waiting for doom's day.

This same end-of-the-world stuff was practiced at school, not just with fire drills but with air raid drills as well. We clambered under our desks in the middle of the room looking away from the glass windows that we were told would blow in. Folks built bomb shelters and stored food in their cellars. One drill had us all filing into the basement of the school, pressing in close to the great center posts that held up the whole building. We got it at home, we got it at school, but the worst was at church. Here the fear went into overdrive.

There was a man, the Reverend Evangelist Harold Gretzinger who specialized in these informative scare-your-pants-off services. He used very impressive charts and graphs stretched on easels across the front of the church. They were basically historical time lines illustrating, with the use of the Holy Bible, the end of the world. Key issues were Israel about to become a nation, which did occur in 1948, the person Hitler as anti-Christ and the atomic bomb as the means by which the moon would turn to blood.

Now at seven or eight years of age I knew I would never go to high school. The White Sox would never win a World Series, and I would lie under a desk in a vapor of steam and blood pouring from the heavens, with a goose-stepping Adolph Hitler marching under my viaduct with my house his first stop. Of course, no one but Mom would be there, poor thing, to have her demise delivered by the mad man. I can see the Reverend Gretzinger walking back and forth with his yardstick pointer slapping the huge charts to make his point, and with every slap half the church members would jump a foot off their pews while the other half would want ever so dearly to dive under theirs.

This was the end-of-the-world atmosphere in which I was raised. A God of love and control was nowhere in sight. Even my viaduct seemed

inadequate here, because the vapor of these ra-
dioactive bombs went everywhere. How do you
plan for the future? What hope is there for accom-
plishment? What difference does school make anyway? It seemed the bad would win out over the
good. So many mixed signals. So frightening. Of
course, children in all of Europe were really ex-
periencing the end of their world, yet we were as
well. So much of our world centered around the
event. We drew planes in warfare and played with
soldiers made of hard rubber. All we could do was
wait … wait … wait.

But the bombs never came. And we experienced VE Day, then VJ Day. And we won. And
my mom ran in the street with all the other neighbors banging pans together celebrating these
monumental days. The boys came home. I saw
them in uniform on the church platform in all their
battle ribbons. People cried, and so did I.

The Reverend Gretzinger didn't come so much
any more. Then he stopped all together. Who does
a child believe anyway, and what can he know
for sure? These early experiences that were so vivid
made lasting impressions on my learning and moral
foundations.

But the trains still ran and my viaduct still stood.
No more blackouts. I heard Hitler was dead. I guess
no one knows anything for sure. I pounded on
the viaduct posts and walls. It was for sure. But
what was there to pound on, in my head. **Where**

was faith? Who knew for sure? The seeds of that deadly plant were sown by the fear peddlers of my childhood, and to this day, I still reap the crop. A child living in fear in a big city marked for destruction is a terrible thing. I tremble even now at the thought of me lying on my little bed staring at the ceiling of our bedroom with the lights out and sirens crying in the city's night. The bombs were so big and I was so small.

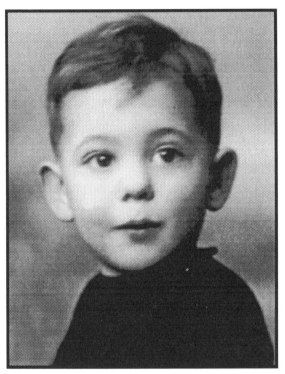

So young, so innocent

Chapter Nineteen
SOUL DEPTH

SOUL DEPTH

ALL CHILDREN HAVE A SENSE of the religious. With me it was directly related to the size of things. Cities like Chicago have a lot of large things by their very nature. Buildings, multi-level boulevards, coal trucks, draft horses pulling garbage wagons, junk wagons and milk wagons. Policemen, at times, rode huge, magnificent animals that shook their mighty bodies in a terrible tremble that seemed to make the earth quake. Fire trucks. Bridge works of iron with fist-sized rivets. Stockyards so large you could smell them miles away when the wind was right. But to me the largest and grandest was the sky at night. I was dwarfed and, frankly, frightened by it all. Of course, it was from this sky, I was told, the German planes would someday fly, and the bomb that would blow the world to smithereens was aimed at Chicago. We lived with blackouts and with wardens wearing official helmets and arm bands ensuring that the city was dark, street by street. To use a common word of the day, crime-in-Italy, it was enough to scare the pee-wadden out of you!

And up there somewhere was God, who was a man in a white robe sitting on a huge chair watching we ants infest this marble of his called earth. I'd lie on my back and just stare up at the size of the sky and wonder about Him. The Catholic/Protestant thing was very confusing. Matters of religion and eternity did cross my mind much more than one would think.

I went to my grandfather's funeral, my mother's dad, whom I did not know. He had been in a home for the mentally ill, I learned long years later. He loved to sit on the railroad tracks, and it was feared he would be mutilated by tons of iron some day, so they packed him off to a "home," whatever that was. I never went there. Strange, my fascination with trains as well, isn't it? I saw him in the box and watched them close the silk-lined lid on his face. I felt sick about that. Then off to the graveyard in a parade of cars I can barely remember. The attendants lowered the casket into a hole in the ground with ropes and threw the loose ends in after it. Then their white gloves were sent sailing down, down, down, as well. I can, to this day, hear the first clods of dirt hit the top of the casket as some of the muffled weeping broke out into sobs here and there. Words were spoken by powerful and eternal people. Who they were was quite beyond me.

What I do remember of a burial in Chicago as a little boy was the shifting of my little oxford shoes in the leaves. I remember my mother's body shaking as I held on to her leg. I remember the awful feeling of a man being buried in dirt, locked up in a box. I remember the great white clouds just hanging there in the sky watching, this whole strange and sickening event. It was the first time I comprehended growing up. My whole world view changed. My line of sight, previously at about the level of a man's hip pocket, was elevated. My world was a very big place, with a very real thing in it, called me. I was facing immortality. I wanted to throw up, but I couldn't find the trigger.

When we got home, I slid my back down the side of the upright piano and sat in the corner of the living room between it and the wall. My mother found me as the autumn summer afternoon gave way to the end of that bright fall day. I was all mixed up inside. The sound of the great train thundering by only intensified my trauma. She asked me, "Charles, why are you sitting there like that?" She knelt down and held my face in her hands looking into my little black eyes set deep in my little face. I can feel her hands, smelling of Jergens lotion, and see the last of that day's autumn summer sun streaming through the dusty lace curtains that covered our front windows. I can remember the dust particles suspended like slow-moving, miniature, transparent diamonds, hanging without number in the air. The whole moment was waiting for a response. So, clearly and softly I responded, "Mama, today made my 'think' hurt."

It was the best I could do with my first encounter with death and the spiritual train tracks that drift off till they merge in infinity. It was the most painful moment of my life, and still is. The thunder in my head had given way to the silence in my heart. A place where Mother's hands couldn't reach. She, of course, was processing her own grief. What would a four-year-old comprehend anyway? What a shallow question. What a bottomless need so overlooked.

I wish now this could have happened in the country. It's only a notion I have. That day the houses were too close together and the train rattling over the tracks did interfere. My mind, or my "think," had stumbled into my soul and I did not, could not, know how deep it really was.

Chapter Twenty
THISTLE GRAY

THISTLE GRAY

THISTLE GRAY. Yep! That was the color. It was Friday evening and we were all at the table when my dad carried in a heavy bag of the unknown. With it still unopened, he sat down at the supper table, said grace with the stack of five plates before him and then announced, "We're going to paint the car!" What a statement. What an imponderable concept. What did it all mean? After the meal, he spread out on the table the contents of the bag. Many sheets of sandpaper, specially treated rags, a gallon of some kind of chemical preparation and then the cans of paint. Four cans of thistle gray automotive paint and two very special brushes. We would start immediately and by Sunday morning we would drive to church in our gleaming new 1940 four-door thistle-gray Chevrolet.

My mind was swimming with the sight. My church friends were my real and loyal friends as opposed to the neighborhood kids, many of whom were Catholics. Catholics. They were like a disease to my father. He cringed when we pronounced the Creator's name as the Catholics did, "GAHD." Heavy on the "ah" sound. Protestants said

"GAUHD." Theirs rhymed with "odd," ours rhymed with "fraud." Now here was my first early training in prejudice. The way you said God. My first understanding of us and them.

Well, back to the kids of our church and, more importantly, to the cars their folks drove up in. These folks of the church and their kids glided up to the curb to unload. Parking lots and churches hadn't connected yet in Chicago. You parked, as we would say, on the street maybe a block or two away, being careful not to block a driveway or park in front of a fire plug. These were nice cars for this was an affluent church. Cadillacs and LaSalles, Buicks and Packards. And then there was our 1940 Chevrolet, dull and rusted here and there. Can you imagine how my head spun as I dreamed of pulling up to that curb at Sixty-fourth and Eggelston in our gleaming thistle-gray Chevrolet? My heart sailed; I felt like the rich. I belonged at last! We were what we drove, and we would finally be someone.

So to the task we ran the moment our dinner was over that Friday night. First a good wash job. Then the endless sanding. All five of us produced powder as the sheets of sandpaper rubbed away our embarrassment. We worked late into the night. Early Saturday morning we were at it again. So many little hard-to-reach places. Of course, we removed no chrome since we did not have the tools to remove or replace it. But Dad had that all figured out. Saturday seemed to fly by.

Finally, the sanding was declared over. The chemical wipe-down took place, and then the tack rag was wiped carefully over the whole car. Prior to this, all the chrome and glass had been taped off with masking tape and newspaper. What a job of masking and preparing. If you could have seen the way my dad lined the kitchen garbage pail with newspaper, you would have some idea of the skill with which he covered the non-painted areas of this car. Well, it was a little late when the actual painting started. The paint was mixed and re-mixed, and then with the stroke of a Michaelangelo, Dad started to lay the gleaming new finish on our car. It was just plain beautiful. The second coat was applied long after the sun had gone down by the light of the single bulb in our garage. While Dad stroked out the last of the thistle gray, my mom polished off the last of our shoes on the drain board of the sink for church the next day.

Dad got up early on Sunday morning and peeled away the last of the masking tape and paper and pulled the car around in front of the house. When you want to see something badly enough, you can sure enough see it. That car looked like a Rolls Royce to my seven-year-old eyes. It ran better. It seemed smoother. Everyone was looking at us as we eased away from the curb in our newly painted chariot. I stood on the hump on the edge of the front seat with my chin resting on the dashboard looking down the expansive sloping front hood. It was so beautiful. My heart raced as I thought of my friends at the church watching us roll up in this thistle-gray, one-of-a-kind concept car. We were going to be someone among the grand automobiles of the day. We turned off Sixty-third Street and then over the one block to the church. There they were right out on the sidewalk as my dad eased us up to the curb. I couldn't, at first, understand the reaction of the older boys. It appeared for all the world as if they were laughing. As we emerged, what appeared to be was. In fact, the laughter was so consuming some of them had fallen to the lawn in near convulsions. And now from the curb, I could see the whole thing for what it really was. It was a car painted like a barn, a thistle-gray barn. Of course, the brush marks were there for all the world to see, and the chrome had paint on most of its upper and lower edges.

I asked, "What's so funny?"

One of them blurted out, "You actually painted your car with a brush!" Of course, I knew nothing of spray guns or proper automotive painting at age seven. What I did know was that we looked like fools, and the beautiful Cadillac that motored up behind us made the disparity painfully obvious. My dad seemed impervious to the whole lot of them. That's where he and I were different.

There's more to this story. As time went by and the hot summer sun beat down on our car, a strange phenomenon occurred. It began to change colors. That thistle gray went into hues of blue and red. We looked like an American flag on wheels. I hated that car. It was the most foolish thing I ever had to ride in. It seemed we kept that car for about 100 years. I can't remember what we traded for or ever rode in again during those years. It was, however, a vivid memory of a dream, born, fulfilled and then destroyed all within about a three-day span. To me, that thistle gray chameleon of a car is a bitter memory of comparative economic standings. I didn't like being poor. The poor should live and worship with the poor. At least, when you're young.

But, bless God, my dad tried and let us all get involved in the dream. It was on the way home that Sunday that my dad must have tried to compensate for the ordeal. While standing next to him on the hump on the edge of the front seat, he asked me, "Charles, would you like to shift?" I jumped at the chance and put my hand on the shift lever that protruded from the right side of the steering column. I can still feel that ivory-like smooth handle in my little hand. I had watched so many times, I knew when and where it went. Often Dad had let me lay my hand on his as he went through the three forward gears. And I did it that day. Down and in. Up and out. Down and out. One, two, three. Stop signs and stop lights allowed the whole thing to repeat. I learned a lot that day in that hand-brushed, painted Chevrolet. In more ways than one, I learned to shift for myself.

Chapter Twenty-One
MELDING WITH GOD

MELDING WITH GOD

I HAVE ALWAYS GONE TO CHURCH. I mean always. I attended regularly for nine months prior to my birth. After that, I went at least three times a week. Sunday morning, Sunday evening and Wednesday night for Prayer Meeting. We drove or took the street car. We had to transfer twice to get to the corner of Sixty-fourth and Eggelston, walking the block from Sixty-third Street. The church was a huge brick structure with massive front steps, a grand horseshoe auditorium with a balcony all around and great lights that illuminated the edifice. The exit signs were gas signs, lit by long taper holders with wooden handles and a fixture on the end to turn on the valve. By only closing my eyes for a moment, I can see those flickering, red-glowing signs, even now, over every door. They were mysterious in this miraculous place.

The pulpit was a marvel. It was of oak. The kind of oak with a lot of grain in it. It was centered on the platform, a theological statement about the centrality of the Bible in the minds and hearts of these believers. It had a huge square base from which rose a grand single-fluted column upon which rested the great sacred desk. It had history.

Mighty hands had gripped the outer edges of that desk. The very founders of the Church of the Nazarene denomination as well as its most illustrious preachers and personalities had preached there.

Dr. L.A. Reed was the pastor there when I was five. He used a wonderfully large gilt-edged pulpit Bible to preach from. He would walk to "The Book," then turn to the text of his sermon, turning those big pages. They fanned the air like the hands of God. We sat in the balcony to the left of the pulpit at about the 30-yard line, so I had a wonderful view of the man, the Book and the waiting flock which numbered close to 1,000.

By the way, his daughter played the organ. It was a Hammond organ. I was to learn in later years that real church organists considered this instrument not a real organ, sort of a dance-hall machine. What a stir Beth caused the first time she slipped onto the organ bench wearing ear rings. This was a no-jewelry kind of place.

L.A. Reed was a mighty preacher. I had no concept of his schooling or skills of delivery. All I knew was that he scared the hell out of me on a regular basis. This was a real hell, of real fire, like when you burned a big pile of leaves on the street in the fall. I mean Hell was being right in the middle of that pile of burning leaves, except it was explained that this was a place where the "fire was never quenched and the worm dieth not." I had no earthly clue what the worms had to do with Hell, but I sure understood that fire business.

In my little heart was a desire to know God. The big God who was even greater than the locomotives with their thunder that so thrilled me under the viaduct. Now when God thundered during a storm, that was thunder from which all other thunder originated. I was afraid of Him but wanted to know Him. That collision of thoughts remains to this day.

One Sunday night for some reason my dad and I wound up sitting on the very front seat of the main floor right in line with the pulpit and, eventually, with Dr. L.A. Reed. (L.A. Reed. Lots of preachers back then had only letters for names. L.A., C.B., S.S., A.S., to name a few that I knew of.) That night he uncorked a beauty of a sermon. My heart was pounding so hard, I felt it would fall out on the floor and just bounce around down there. The "altar call" was given and folks were invited to "come forward" and pray. Several did, and I knew it was what I was to do. The distance from that front curved oak pew to the rounded altar rail, with its kneeling pad that followed the great arc of the platform, seemed to be a thousand miles away. I was so little. My heart was pounding so hard. I so wanted to know God and, as preachers and Sunday school teachers put it, "let Jesus into my heart." I was frightened beyond measure. Hell and fire waited beyond the flickering exit sign above every door. Every door of exit made you pass under the fire. I was so caught in the middle between my fear and my need. There was no one to help me. I was only five. No one saw the tears rolling down my face dripping on my little cowboy shirt. My head was bowed staring at the floral carpet at my feet. The emotion intensified with repeated verses of the invitational song sung by the whole congregation. Suddenly, I knew everybody was looking at me. Waiting for me. I moved in closer to my dad's leg, my eyes level with his pockets. He always held the song book with one hand high in the air and tipped his head back, like he had a stiff neck, to take advantage of his bifocals.

It was as though I melted in a slow-turning motion. Like a skater going into a spin in extreme slow motion. I just turned. My stomach and side rubbed the front edge of the pew as I turned until I faced the whole crowd, of course, hidden by the height of the pew back. It's then that I slid to my knees and laid my wet face on the seat of that dark old oak pew. I screwed my little fists into my little eyes and wept as if my child's heart would break. Eventually, my dad realized what was going on. I don't remember what he said, but I do remember what I had done. I had sort of turned and melded with God. I so wanted Him to be there, and He was.

I was never to be the same again. I did not

know how to relate to what had happened. It was almost an experiential event without any explanation attached. I mean, I was five. What could I know? The fact of the matter was, evidently, I knew enough. My heart had preceded my brain by many years.

It has not been until these later years that I have begun to understand the gravity of that event. Prevenient Grace. The grace of God that goes before understanding. Now, somehow, the thunder over and in my head and the real thunder were connected. How? That's a question I'm still trying to answer. The melting created melding. There's so much understanding still to thaw. But I remember clearly the night it all began to melt.

Chapter Twenty-Two
THE THUNDER IN MY HEAD

THE THUNDER IN MY HEAD

YOU'VE HEARD IT SAID that if you live next
to trains you grow to not hear them at all. To a
point that's true. I don't remember being awak-
ened by the B & O that crossed the viaduct only
two houses from ours. I got to where I didn't hear
it or feel it, though it did shake the ground. But,
of course, that's nonsense because you hear what
is there to be heard whether you realize it or not.
The ear drum, the auditory nerves and their connection to the brain all function. Beyond this, these
sound experiences pass over the subliminal level
of the brain and are recorded in the subconscious.
I have come to learn that what you're not listening to when you listen to whatever you're listening to is the most effective input in your future
influence. The ears of my conscious were plugged,
but the thunder was pouring in. Train after train,
day and night, for the first several years of my life.
Powerful, amplified sounds of huge engines pump-
ing the great pistons and belching the black smoke
as it passed, pulling the ever present coal car and
a long line of rattling box cars that set up a hyp-
notic rhythm on the tracks, echoing through the
viaduct morning, noon and night. Remember, I

heard this from infancy until my age reached double digits. That sound, I believe, affected me, beyond any doubt. It affected my mind, and I mean in my mind.

Alluded to previously in this book, at about five years of age I started to experience a phenomenal mental response that was emotional in nature. I've told very few people about it, and have never written about it until now. The phenomena continued until I was in my mid-twenties. The best way to describe them is that they were spells. They were terrifying. To this day I don't know why I never told anyone about them until I was in my early forties. The word that best describes this experience is amplification. Sound was louder, light was brighter, color was more vivid, movement was much faster, etc. It was terribly frightening. Years later, I visited some of the great caverns of the world. Among the dripping stalactites in this deep lower earth the guide would ask for silence and the lights would be turned out. In that near eternal darkness of spatial endlessness the guide would clap two hands together only once. The sound that "up top" would be almost unnoticed, down there would be deafening as it echoed deep into the abyss, increasing in terror and eternal-like importance. And those are the operative words, "eternal-like importance." This was going on in my little head. Small at first, growing in intensity until I felt as if the phenomenon would replace my own personal reality. This was very powerful and frothing with horror.

My medical doctor son who is a student of the mind cannot really explain it. In spite of his medical degree and psychiatric training at a world-class center, he can only peer into the eyes of his dad whom he dearly loves and wonder where and how the experience came. I know. **It was the trains.**

Everyone has trains in their early life. They are the repetitious experiences that formed life-long responses that you live with to this day. They are the origins of fears, joys and beliefs. Of course, the B & O Railroad was only the megaphone of my other life issues. Thunder, you know, is the result of colliding air. It is the effect, not the cause. The fact of the matter really is that we all live with effects. This is not about my adult life, so I will not elaborate on the ramifications of these experiences in my later years. The cause was over my head. This is not about trains, but it is. The effect has been in my head. You don't hear the trains when you live next to the tracks ... but, believe me, you do!

My dad, mom, twin brother and me

Chapter Twenty-Three
MY FATHER'S LEG

MY FATHER'S LEG

YOU NEED TO KNOW about my father's leg. His left leg to be exact. He was born in California near San Francisco at the time of the great quake in '06. In deference to my grandfather's health, they moved to the drier air of New Mexico where he died anyway. About this time my father contracted tuberculosis that settled in his left leg. He was a pre-schooler at the time. His mother, my grand-mother, packed up my dad and his older sister and headed for Chicago to find work to sustain her two children and herself. This she did in mod-erate style.

My grandmother was a severe woman, to me, who lived in a little dark house with a compost pile (whatever that was) in the backyard. She cor-rected your English and manners, how you sat or wore your shirt or blew your nose. She lived a hard life during the depression and the years lead-ing up to it, in part, due to my father's left leg. Numerous times surgeons advised that it be am-putated, but she prevailed in preventing that course of action. My dad spent most of his young life in Chicago in a T.B. sanitarium. Fresh air was the cure-all in those days. He slept in large dorm rooms with other boys with piles of blankets over them with the windows wide open to the Chicago elements; often drifts of snow were left under the window sills on the floor in the morning.

Granted, my father must have questioned this turn of events in his young life, but none of it ever weakened his mind. Though he never earned $10,000 a year, gross salary, he almost completed a degree in mechanical engineering at the Illinois Institute of Technology. He became a master mechanic, chief tool designer and a brilliant draftsman. He never played any sports. None. That was to become a great loss to me. He loved music and played in the Linbloom High School band. The cornet. Not the trumpet! (Trumpets were a jazz instrument, light years removed from John Philip Sousa.) He could fix anything, and he did so most often in the basement. I can still hear his one bad leg bumping down the stairs of the basement, stiff and small — thump, thump, thump, it came. I questioned the leg as a little boy who had two good legs. I saw his leg in a state of undress only a few times while at the beach on the shore of Lake Michigan in Jackson Park. The sight was unforgettable. It was scarred where corrective surgery had taken place and so thin all the way up. He could bend the knee about ten degrees. I know it hurt him in cold weather because he put a sock affair around it and grimaced when he took a first step. From my vantage point, I was just above eye level with that knee and saw it at all times when he was near. I felt sorry for my dad and hated all the fun he must have missed. I just sort of understood why we didn't play catch or handle bats or own gloves. These are things that I instinctively loved and bought or traded for on my own. He bought a trombone for me in time and we had a family band: two cornets, a clarinet and a trombone all set up in the living room. Sempre Fidelis and Stars and Stripes Forever filled the house after a fashion. I wanted to be filling a net with basketballs, throwing cross-body blocks and cracking bats on the red threads of hard balls. Well, that was to be years later, and I guess it was the best he had to offer. My music, honestly, has served me well in my adult life, but I still resent that leg that tripped so many of my childish dreams.

I believe my dad realized my silent heartache though we never really talked about it but once. My brother and I were little guys just noticing the White Sox and Cubs in the *Chicago Daily News* as well as the Bears and the Cardinals in the fall. I didn't comprehend the Black Hawks because no one played hockey where we lived. I couldn't read the words of the paper, but I would lie on the floor and pour over the pictures. The sport page was always discarded by Dad right off, and the "funnies" as well.

I'm sure Dad felt the deficiency of his sportlessness and made a stab at explaining it to my twin brother and me. Sitting us down on the upright piano bench in the living room, he stood over us and patted that left leg. I'll never forget his explanation that I'm sure he believed until the day he died.

"Boys," he said, "God allowed me to get T.B. in this left leg. Now God is fair and He, in His mercy, gave me you two twin boys to make up for it." He patted our heads as if he were covering us with his glory. We were the real life embodiment of the mercy of God.

I sat under the viaduct a long time that day as the sun set and the lightning bugs began to ignite. Me, Charles Ray Millhuff, one-half of God's replacement for a stiff leg. Believe me, a lot of thunder went over my head that night, and some of it still rumbles in the distance.

The good old summertime

Chapter Twenty-Four
HOW FALSE; HOW TRUE

HOW FALSE; HOW TRUE

FEELING IMPORTANT comes a little later in a child's life. The burr haircut of summer to the bundled-up look of winter are purely functional at five and six. They become really weird at 15 and 16. What I looked like was of no concern to my conscious mind as a little boy. Why, even dirt was of no consequence. Mother bathed my brother and me in the same bath water, one after the other. I can still smell the pinkish-red Lifebuoy soap and see the darkening gray water. Clean had no real significance to me. I know now it was a part of health, but I didn't know then. Then it was a huge part of inconvenience. My days were spent in what Mom set out for me, selected from a painted chest of drawers in a shared bedroom with my brother and sister. Bunk beds were on one wall for my brother and me, a single bed for my sister, three years older, on the other. Feelings about her, by us, were so strong that we might as well have been separated by the Great Wall of China.

During the week it was corduroys or overalls, but on Sunday it was a pair of gabardine slacks and a tan two-tone cowboy shirt, a belt with a silver buckle and the well-worn but polished oxfords with perforated toe caps. The shirt was open at the neck with the collar points reaching almost to our shoulders. I say ours because my twin brother and I wore the same thing week in and week out until we approached our early teens. We graduated from grade school in matching double-breasted blue serge suits bought at a discount clothing store, Robert Halls. These were the first suits we had ever owned or worn. All those years we wore the same old, same old. Our twinness far exceeded our individual personhood.

One Sunday, without my brother, I was invited to go out with the Whitsells for the Sunday noon meal. Doctor Faye Whitsell was an eminent eye surgeon in the Chicago area. We were going to his club. We arrived on the scene which was splendorous to say the least. The great expanse of the golf course surrounded the clubhouse in gleaming green glory. I had never seen a lawn like this before. Tucked in one corner was an enormous swimming pool and patches of tennis courts with their nets taut and ready for play.

I was rather astounded with the place. We mounted the grand entrance steps and stood in the chandeliered lobby. We were announced, and preparations were made. It was as the table was being readied for the Whitsells along with their son, Dick, my friend, and the rest of the party that the problem began to develop. I was so gee-gaw at the surroundings that it never dawned on me that I was the center of attention or, as it turned out, distraction. It was explained that the Beverly Hills Country Club was a coat-and-tie-only place and that the cowboy shirt tucked into the worn gabardine slacks were lacking both tie and coat, two items of clothing I had never owned in my entire life.

Can an eight-year-old feel embarrassment? Yes! Do these citadels of pomp and circumstance make allowances? No! Here I was holding up the whole works. Dr. Faye and Betty Whitsell, sons David and Dick were all decked out in proper attire as well as the other invited guests from the church. That kind of attention is painful to say the least. I felt both poor and stupid. A tie was borrowed from a waiter. A coat materialized with the sleeves rolled up. It hung below my knees like a robe. I looked like Charlie Chaplin, the "little tramp."

We were ushered finally into the grand expanse of the dining room, which appeared to accommodate thousands of children dressed in the perfect attire from Marshall Field's Department Store, a store I was to learn of years later. The meal was beyond my wildest comprehension. The entire event exceeded my reach and grasp: goblets of crystal, chargers under the dinner plates, forks and spoons of silver, and starched napkins placed by a waitress in my lap.

It was an oversight on the part of the Whitsells.

Dick blew it off like a joke, but I didn't. That stuck in my young brain like an ice pick. One day I would be in a position to never be embarrassed like that again.

Today my clothes are very current and often expensive. Here was the genesis of it all. That ill-fitting coat hangs on my back to this day, with the black tie cinched around my now bunched-up tan cowboy shirt collar. I shudder at the remembrance.

I am often asked these days how I've learned to dress like I do. Do I have a designer or do I pour over books of style or fashion? No, not really. I had the reverse of style burned into my little eight-year-old heart in a place I didn't belong — but somehow I did. And today I do.

Clothes suddenly became a part of my persona. It is, granted, a shallow issue but deep enough to touch my heart. What he wears, to a point, makes the man. That day it made the boy, and he was never the same again. A day I will never forget. It was the day I learned how important costumes are in the play of life. You're right, Mr. Shakespeare, "all of life is a stage," especially at the Beverly Hills Country Club on the south side of Chicago. Feeling important, I learned, had a lot to do with what you have on you, not what you have in you. How false. How true. The conundrums of reality. I embraced it at eight.

Chapter Twenty-Five
CORDUROY

CORDUROY

I **LIKE THE FEEL** of corduroy to this day. A pair of navy blue corduroy bib overalls were my favorite attire as a child. Without shirts in the summer and with a flannel, long-sleeve shirt in the winter. Corduroy has a feel to it. You can rub it with reward. The reward is memory. It was texture beyond the ordinary. I can scratch it in my mind and feel the rippling of it pass beneath my little nails on the ends of my little fingers.

The way things feel is remarkably important to a five-year-old. The cold porcelain of a kitchen table top. The rough bark of an old tree. The shiny paper of a *look* magazine. The soft fuzz of your summer burr haircut. The fake fur on your mom's mouton winter coat. The slippery shine on the hood of your dad's just polished car. The squeaky feel of a plate in the rinse dishwater at the sink. The feel of the bricks your house is built of. The cold, real tile floor of the little front door entrance. The ripple of the bed posts over each shoulder in bed. The cement posts of the viaduct shuddering as the thunder of a train goes over your head. What you feel is so much a part of your young life.

The problem is you can't wear corduroy on

your heart. It's just in there writing away madly, on your memory, as life happens. I mean, I guess, your heart. Where as in most other experiences I touched things with my little heart, in the most important things, they touched me. What were they? They were the eyes of people. The facial expressions. The way they physically touched me. Being backed into at the A&P by some lady even though you're trying to hide behind your mom next to the Campbell's soup display. It's being pulled by an ear or your hair or your arm. It hurts your heart, not your ear or hair or arm. And then in those moments there's no corduroy to put on your heart to feel with your deepest emotions.

Do you notice how men, as they grow older, love to wear corduroy when plain cotton or wool would do? It's the memory of those corduroy ribs and your little legs inside that wonderful stuff. It's miracle material. I can, right now, see my legs with my knees dug into the dirt at the curb under the viaduct playing with my red dump truck. I wipe my hands on the bib part of the outfit. It's fall and the cloth is warm as I play in the shadows. Some of the cords are worn away on the knees. They are tan now in color with metal buckles at the top where the straps attach to the bib. They smell so good when Mom takes them off the line all full of the aroma of Oxydol. Folded and put in a wicker basket, Mom brings them to my room and puts them in the painted bureau that is mine. I dig them out in the morning and pull them on like second skin.

But I grew out of them, and then others, and then the whole idea. But as I write this, they seem very real again some 50 years later. I guess I can put them on my heart after all. I close my eyes, and without moving a hand I feel it again and all that's wrapped up in it. It's just corduroy.

Chapter Twenty-Six
SHOES

SHOES

I LOOK AT THE FOOTWEAR kids own these days, and I marvel. Athletic shoes today are developed by and for the greatest athletes in the world. A child becomes a man by just lacing them onto his feet. The $100-plus price tag guarantees that these are not near replicas but exact replicas of the bigger models.

When I was a little boy, I had one pair of shoes. They were Buster Brown oxfords with a scalloped toe piece and lots of little holes punched in the borders. They were brown. What fun to stand in the X-ray machine at the shoe store and look at my feet outlined by the nails of the new shoes. There were my bones. Lots of bones and all in my feet. There were two viewing scopes. One for me, one for my folks. I guess people's feet started falling off, because the X-ray idea died off about the same time people started thinking aluminum pans caused cancer.

Look at the way a person is standing, and it will tell you a lot about how they are feeling. I often stood with one shoe on top of the other. I would screw my right toe into the floor or ground when I was nervous. My feet would jump a lot —

most of the time the only escape for my untamed energy. These shoes kicked cans and rocks and tripped on curbs and broken sidewalks. They were polished with a liquid polish every Saturday night for church the next day. The polish came in a tall bottle with a cap that was attached to a twisted wire with a cotton ball dauber on the end.

How I wanted a pair of real gym shoes: high tops with a black rubber spot on the ankles. Or wonder of wonders, some high tops with a knife pocket and buckled top straps over the calf.

I can see my shoes to this day. I can hear them as the soles flapped when the front sewing wore through. I remember my dad gluing them together. I really hated those shoes. I never cross my legs and look at my fine Bostonian wing tips without remembering the first wing tips I ever purchased as a late teen. How it all comes around. I hated those shoes but never felt bad about them. I'll tell you why.

Every Saturday night, as I've already said, my mom would polish the shoes. First a piece of newspaper was laid out on the kitchen counter. Then the shoes were lined up. My dad's included. His were safety-toed, which meant they had a steel cap under the leather of the toe. These were polished for Sunday as well. We all went to church in the one pair of shoes we each owned. We were a one-pair family! I bet my dad hated his as badly as I hated mine. We should have talked about things like that, but we didn't. Didn't seem to be the thing to do.

I've got a closet full of shoes today. They're all just sitting there, wide open to desolation. Not a shoe tree in sight. But not my dad's steel-toed safety shoes. Shoe trees. Great cedar shoe trees right in 'em the minute they came off his feet before he slipped into his corduroy slippers.

I have a lot of mixed feelings about my shoes and why I polish them so much. Why I never throw them out. Why I look at them so much. When you looked at yourself, that's where you started, at your feet. They might as well be on my feet right now, and that was 50 years ago. Scuffed, broken laces knotted back into service. Poor droopy socks. They walked in gravel and on cement and kicked footballs and slid into second base. They went to church and school and under the bed at night.

I wish I could wear 'em one more time, and walk into my viaduct with that red dump truck under my arm. Just one more time. Life is so much more simple with only one pair of shoes. One pair of Buster Brown oxfords. It wasn't all bad after all.

The year the viaduct was built

Chapter Twenty-Seven
PROTECTION

PROTECTION

IN 1940 THERE WAS VERY LITTLE in the way of child protection. No childproof drug containers. No child car seats or seat belts for that matter. Lots of lead in all the paint, and our attic was knee deep in asbestos insulation. The water had no fluoride and our feet were exposed to blasts of radiation when we poked them into the X-ray machine at the shoe store. One fear I really remembered was a real fear of polio. Drinking fountains and the wading pool at Marquette Park were off limits during the hottest months. I was fairly unprotected from the elements and the realities of physical life. But what of the interior places you could not fence in or sterilize or build a safety railing around?

I seemed to be so frightened on the inside. I distinctly remember hiding behind my mother's dress and holding one of her legs at the A&P in numerous situations. I was most frightened of Catholic nuns. Their faces framed in plaster, all puffy with the eyes of God. Those long layered robes tied at the waist with knotted ropes. I knew these were for beating children or tying them up or even worse. The butcher with his knives flying in mid-air in perfect rhythm as they were sharpened on the "steel." The coffee grinder or the big latch on the cooler door banging shut with its huge hinges. I was fascinated with the stock boy as he ripped open cardboard cartons and stamped on the boxes or the can lids with an ink pad and adjustable price stamper flying from can to can like a machine gun. He had them on the shelf and was attacking the next layer before one could catch one's breath. I wanted to do that one day, and while a student in college I did.

I have been told that the only fears we know are the ones we've been taught. I believe that's true. Therefore, most of them are perceived. Though perceived, they are painful — very painful for a little boy of four or five years of age. I don't remember a protector. Soon teachers frightened me. Policemen frightened me. Certain neighbors were to be avoided at all cost, because they frightened me. I trembled a lot on the inside. There was no place to hide. No one to go to. Where was my older sister or twin brother? How about my mom or dad? Why did I feel so vulnerable? The city itself is such a big, loud place. So much danger. Death seemed so imminent. Then the atomic bomb when I was six. I heard at church the world would surely end, and at school we were taught to crawl under our desks in the event of an atomic bomb attack. We practiced and practiced.

Well, the only safe place, of course, was the viaduct. It, after all, could support a train. No bomb was greater than a steam engine. And the noise. The wonderful noise. The earth-trembling thunder of it all. All sounds were obliterated in this orchestration of safety. Isn't that strange that a coffee grinder grinding up 8 O'clock coffee beans in a red coffee grinder machine at the A&P was infinitely more frightening than 100 tons of iron and steel and steam thundering over my head? It was my protection. When it was there, it was supreme. It was omnipotent, all powerful, all protective.

Fear follows a child like a dark shadow and bangs on into the adult years. Only the very smart or very brave find other viaducts. Where was God? I didn't know except I feared Him the most. God's headquarters were in cities; big cities like Chicago. He worked downtown, wherever that was. I never knew Him as protector. I didn't know anyone as protector. Ralph Nader was not on the scene yet, and Dr. Spock was not in vogue.

Little boys need viaducts, and I had one. Only two doors down. So much steel and concrete. So eternal and real. My protection. And even in bed, following a good beating, I knew it was there. I could go into my mind. The steam, the huff, huff, huff of the engine and the occasional whistle was the deity in my life. If only I could have taken the viaduct to the A&P where the nuns and the butcher were. But alas, I could not. Mother's leg and I behind her "house dress" had to do. It was what I hung on to.

Protection is a wonderful word! It should be softer than concrete and quieter than steam pistons and giant rolling steel wheels over the breaks in the tracks. It should be arms and being tightly held in an elevated hug, or a sister's "This is my little brother!" But it wasn't. And the city was so big and scary. And I was so small. Protection. Protection is a wonderful word.

Chapter Twenty-Eight
STARTING POINTS

STARTING POINTS

IT HAD REAL SWOOPY FENDERS that today remind you of the "DECO" era. It was red and a little larger than a small boy's lap. It was a tin toy dump truck that I received on Christmas morning when I was about five. It had wooden wheels and a bed that tilted and dumped its contents through a swinging tailgate. It was a wonderful toy. Undoubtedly, the best toy I ever owned. I spent untold hours playing with that truck, typically under the viaduct, moving dirt and stones and building imaginary structures of immense size. With a train thundering overhead and my truck loaded full and overflowing, I was in the midst of my own global industrial world. It was bigger and grander and louder than I could ever express. So many days along the curb of that viaduct, in one of the many hundreds of neighborhoods of Chicago, were filled with these grandiose projects that still ring in splendor in my memory. No television to watch. No radio for kids at 10 o'clock in the morning. Hot! Hot! Hot! inside the house. Here was the place to be. But also here was the place I fell in love with machinery in general, and cars and trucks in particular.

Riding in the front seat of our car was this experience to the tenth power. This 1940 Chevy four-door in 1944 was built long before seat belts and shoulder restraints and certainly child seats. I sat on the edge of the wool-covered seat of that old Chevy with my chin on the dash board and my eyes riveted to the dials and gauges. "What's that?" I'd ask over and over. My dad who was a mechanical engineer found common ground here with his youngest son, and had no loss of enthusiasm for the project of educating me along the lines of all things automotive. Now my red dump truck, with the swoopy fenders, took substance as my dad guided the car along the brick paved main streets and thoroughfares of Chicago's south side. These streets were often inlaid with sets of street-car tracks that were as slippery as ice when wet, or so my dad told me. Here we would talk about speedometers and gas gauges, ammeters and oil pressure as well as odometers and high beam indicator lights. All this was centered behind the steering wheel in a cluster of wonder which glowed at night like a rocket ship. Standing on the hump that covered the manual transmission, Dad would let me hold on to that big inner horn-ringed steering wheel with my little left hand and feel the turn of the wheel as the flying lady hood ornament flew in the intended direction. What power; what control. At about age seven, I learned to shift in the "H" pattern from first through third after Dad had depressed the clutch pedal that activated wonderful things under the very bump I was standing on. Soon, I was steering and shifting all at once, with my mother grinding her teeth in stark fear in the back seat as my sister described our family's inevitable fiery death in a mass of steaming steel and rubber. At seven, I almost drove the car. In Chicago. At seven.

That act, repeated many hundreds of times, was quite possibly the greatest trust and affirmation my dad ever gave me. He let me drive at seven in a city of millions. Was that a foolish thing to do? Of course, it was. Was it the right thing to do? Of course, it was. Here was the foolish and the right merging in my little mind, originated by God, who at that age for everybody is one's dad. It's so clear. The windshield wiper switch on top of the dash in dull gray plastic. The radio grill. The clock embedded in the glove compartment door. The glowing dials and the push-out wing windows in the front corners of the doors. Here was such power and responsibility entrusted to me by my dad.

Why in this automotive setting was I never scolded for over-steering or gear-meshing? In all other areas of life, I have a memory of almost unbroken failure, but not in the car. Here Dad and I and the Chevy were one. Here I had respect and ability. Here, as I've said, we had common ground. He was a genius with machinery, I was to later learn. And to some degree, I am as well.

Starting points are hard to find in life. All accomplishments must start. We had one and didn't know it. It shines in my childhood memory as one of the brightest starting points of all. Like a farm child who first steers the tractor or holds the reins of a team of horses. Here I leaned against my dad. It was intimate. It felt good. I needed it. I think he did, too. I eventually sat on his lap and did the whole thing when my legs were long enough. At age 13 my brother and I went on a trip back to New Mexico with my dad to see his father's grave. Across the barren desert lands we, my brother and I, drove hundreds of miles under age and without licenses, breaking the law with glee where the speed limit was posted as reasonable and proper.

It began with a swoopy-fendered red dump truck played with on the street of our south Chicago home. I progressed to a hands-on love affair with things that run and move. But more than this, it was a starting point with my dad. The tragedy is, we didn't know what was happening. I do now. What I wouldn't give for that war era dump truck toy or for one like it. What I wouldn't give to have known then what I know now about starting points. I had so much more in my little left hand than a 1940 Chevrolet steering wheel at seven. I had the handle to my dad's heart. If we only could have known how to point the flying lady. She was my unknown dreams. Our main concern was sliding on the streetcar tracks when we should have been shooting for the stars.

The corner candy store

Chapter Twenty-Nine
IT WAS THE BERRYS

IT WAS THE BERRYS

MY MOTHER MADE ICE CREAM in ice cube trays with the dividers removed. It was a concoction of evaporated milk, sugar and other ingredients that I neither remember or would understand. We never got ice cream out of a box from the store nor did we ever own an ice cream freezer. That seems strange when I think of it, almost un-American. My mom's substitute ice cream was really good to a five- or six-year-old who had nothing to compare it to.

My father was an important committee member at our church and had to occasionally sign documents in conjunction with this job. Mr. Berry was, as far as I knew, the richest man in the church or maybe even the world. He had a leadership role on the church board and would occasionally come to our house to have my dad sign some things. He would call when he was coming. We had one of those stand-up phones that looked like a candlestick with the ear piece hanging on the side. All telephone numbers started with a name in those days. Ours was Hemlock and then some numbers. You only used the first two letters of what was called the exchange preceding the numbers.

I've long since forgotten the numbers of which there were four.

When someone important called, my mom rushed around making her ice cream. One night Mr. Berry called. She went into action. It was mixed in a Mixmaster mixing machine. By the time Mr. Berry's LaSalle glided up to the curb, the mixture was hard and ready. I watched for him from under the viaduct, because he always came that way. I ran after the massive black car past the two houses to where Mr. Berry was being seated at the chipped porcelain table in our kitchen. He preferred the kitchen. He understood food. He owned the Blue Ribbon Mayonnaise Company. Our family of five would sit with Mr. Berry around the table as my mom cut up the ice cream from the ice cube tray and served it to us in bowls that had trees and rabbits painted in the bottom. With the ice cream, we were served Salerno Butter Cookies. They were round and scalloped with a hole in the middle. We kids put our finger in the hole and nibbled around it until all that was left was a little cookie ring, and then we ate that.

Mr. Berry always gave my sister, my brother and me a quarter. That was a whopping amount to a child in that day. When the good humor man came in his truck ringing the row of bells over his windshield, we ran to him or the corner candy store to spend our little fortunes. Two cents for a popsicle, five cents for an orange creamsicle or fudgesicle and a dime for a real ice cream drumstick, the top all covered with nuts. I can so well remember the wonderful things that happened when Mr. Berry came to our house. It really was wonderful. And to me, he might as well have been the King of England.

One night at church following the Sunday evening service my sister informed us of the impossible, the improbable and the unforgettable! We had been invited to the Berrys' home for some, as they called it, "fellowship" after church. We followed the big black LaSalle in our funny little Chevrolet. They lived in Beverly Hills. This was the domain of the very rich, the powerful, neat people, like the Berrys. We wound through the curving streets and finally arrived at the great pillar gate posts of his house. Up the driveway we followed, stopping at the front walk as Mr. Berry pulled into a garage far larger than our house. It had living quarters above it, we were told. I had no idea what that meant. All I could see were quarters with arms and legs. A child, remember, takes things very literally. We walked into the front hall where we hung our coats. It was as big as our living room. And then, into their living room. Now remember, my eyes were at a table-top level. Everything was big to me: this room, the grand piano, the furniture, the pictures. I realize now they really were big. This night will remain burned into my mind forever. This was the first time I had ever seen television. It was a five-inch Muntz console unit. On that television, coming from the Chicago stadium, was a hockey game. It was so real you could feel the sprays of ice in your face right there in that living room. And it was in color. Well, sort of. A plastic sheet of color had been attached to the screen. The top third was sky blue, the middle was flesh tone, and the bottom third was grass green. Here were hockey players with sky-blue heads and flesh-colored Indians on their Black Hawk uniforms, skating on green ice. It was fabulous! It looked so natural. Isn't it interesting how things look so real when you want them to?

We were then ushered into the dining room and to a table loaded down with food. Such an array of meats and cheeses and breads. We were told to make our sandwiches. I needed help, of course, but I could sure point to what I wanted. Mrs. Berry made me a world-class Dagwood monster! Then we moved to the chips and pickles and cokes in ice cold bottles. My older sister gave me a poke and instructed me to, for heaven's sake, ask for mayonnaise. Of course, I couldn't eat half of it but, never mind, this was the way one did things at the Berrys. To top it off, we went to the sideboard loaded down with real ice cream in round cardboard boxes. And to go with the ice cream was hot fudge, butterscotch, nuts and cherries. I staggered to my spot at the table, my eyes swimming in the wonder before me. No ice cube trays or Salerno Butter Cookies here.

It was at that very moment I decided I would not be poor when I grew up. I liked the ice cream out of the round boxes better than the stuff that came out of the ice cube trays. That fact burned deeply into my little brain that night. I mean the whole event literally changed me.

It was always wonderful when Mr. Berry came to our house, but **Wow,** how my life changed when I went to his house. That evening did a lot in me, and I don't mean the sandwiches and the ice cream.

In later years I made a very significant Biblical comparison that has worked its way into my preaching many times through the years. It revolves around a well-known Bible verse from the Revelation of Jesus Christ to Saint John, chapter three, verse twenty:

"Behold I stand at the door and knock; if any man hear my voice and open the door, I will come in to him, and will sup with him, and he with me."

In another place in this book, I tell of the night I knelt at the front pew of our church and opened the door of my five-year-old life to the knocking Christ. He came in and has supped or eaten with me all these years. It has been wonderful to have Him here in my house. But the verse ends by promising that we will one day sup or eat at his house with Him. Now in my mid-50s, that night at the Berrys still remains one of my main metaphoric concepts of heaven. Going to the Berrys' house was sure a different story than Mr. Berry coming to our house, as great as that was.

I don't know for sure, but I doubt that there'll be ice cube tray ice cream in heaven. Just the real thing!

The thunder in my head rolled way off in the distance that night. As I settled into bed that evening, I knew I had seen the rest of the world. Some day those trains that rattled past our house two houses down would take me there. The Berrys had no idea what they served me that night, so many years ago, in the dead cold of a Chicago winter night. Neither did I. I know now what it was. It was the Berrys!

The Viaduct

Chapter Thirty
TAJ MAHAL

TAJ MAHAL

THE ANCHORS OF A CHILD'S LIFE can be buildings. The house, the school, the church, the A&P, the corner candy store, the fire engine house, the fieldhouse at the park and the corner bank, to name a few. In these places are people who put the blood in the bricks.

In the country the anchors are old hay barns and a deserted one-room school house, where the road comes to a Y at the great oak that was split years ago by lightning. And then all the space. Though I saw very little of the country as a child, I saw enough at the outer edges of the city to know the difference between space and no space. When one can't find space without, one goes within. Souls must have room to move and grow and, yes, even breathe. It's the "pent-upness" that fuels frustration in fortresses of brick and iron and cement. It becomes anger.

The thing I liked about the viaduct was that it was open. It was the essence of openness. It had no doors. Yet it had protection, excitement, concealment and strength. It was the most wonderfully built thing in my young life. I can write of many of the things that went on in and around and even under that viaduct in the cool shadows of its great pillars; yet it was the thing, the place, the experience of it, itself, that I do so clearly remember. And indeed, its impact is sharpened by my comparison of it to other buildings. There was a sameness to them all.

Part of the impact here was the doings of a cow in the barn of Mrs. O'Leary. The cow kicked over a lantern in the late 1800s, which started a fire that eventually spread to the whole city and burned it to the ground in one of the worst conflagrations since the great fire of London. When the city finally got back on its feet, it instituted building codes that gave it much of the character that remains even to this day. All brick and mortar construction. All lath and plaster walls. Here and there, and most particularly on the north side of the city, the fascinating deco style of Frank Lloyd Wright was evident in the architecture. By and large, it was the cold red bricks or imposing rough, chiseled, dirty limestone from nearby Indiana that prevailed. To me, it was a cold, imposing, large place filled with the feelings of dungeon-like structures. I'm sure to others there was and is beauty and graceful strength to the whole place.

These are the memories of a child and his visual surroundings and the emotional effect they had on me. House after house built with an identical plan. Same brick. Same roof line. Same three or four feet separating each dwelling. Block after block and neighborhood after neighborhood of these pre- and post-war houses. The post-war homes (1945) went to picture windows in place of the four sash casements that fronted our house. A little stone to break up the brick came into vogue in the fifties, adding a new type of architecture. Any house that was different was a show place. Two-story or "T" or "L" shaped. Of course, there were the homes in Beverly Hills that were true mansions with long driveways and corner turrets and grand side porches with huge garages or stables with servants' quarters above. These were far beyond my scope of realization since we had no cause to ever go there but for the exception mentioned in this book.

Architecture has its own impact on a culture. This is well known. The reverse is probably more accurate. My soul longed for a larger place. I felt closed in. I hate the city to this day, and feel a sense of incarceration whenever I have need to drive among the deep shadows of a large downtown metropolitan city. I don't hear the rhythm of life or see the blending of culture. I roll up the windows, purposely missing the ethnic smells meeting in peaceful union. I feel confined. I did feel confined.

The thing about that viaduct was that it was connected with an enterprise that was going places. It was only rough cement and very common and without imagination; yet, it was a palace of dreams for me. It took a little of the pressure off my in-hibited creativity. The thunder of the trains was larger than the whole suffocating place. Little did I know of California or the fruited plains. The white and green mountains of the northeast, or even the lakes that were hiding in the forest of nearby Wis-consin. How could I?

Damming up a small stream has potential, how-ever. Great ponds become virtual lakes. Eventu-ally these dams can give way or be blown away by education, travel and daring adventure. A Johnstown flood can explode because of the po-tentiality of energy that seemingly negative forces of restraint have created. The Johnstown flood was a horrific national and corporate selfish disaster. What good, if any, came of it? That question has been debated. I can only say that I owe a deep debt of gratitude to the bricks and confinement that were an integral part of the pressure that built up steam in my little boiler. Granted, the city was only one component in the matrix of my eventual adulthood creativity and positive contributions, if there have been any. The negative has been the ensuing anger and accompanying depression that unexplained confinement sees as injustice.

I'm six years old. I feel the sameness that is not me. School desks are bolted in lines to the floor. Red wooden and iron streetcars are confined to tracks deeply embedded in the paver bricks. Cement window sills stretch as far as the eye can see fronting cookie cutter houses. Sidewalks never give way to lanes or paths. Fire hydrants stand like sentinels holding down the asphalt. And then — then there is a viaduct. My viaduct. What a wonderful break in all of this monotony. And the thunder, the earth-shaking thunder, the announcement that ends my hopelessness locked in thought. At six years of age, it was the Taj Mahal.

My twin Howard and me (I'm the one moving) and my sister Marjorie, ages one and four.

EPILOGUE

AN EPILOGUE

I DIDN'T SEE IT COMING. It was 50 years later, and what I didn't see coming was the train. I was flat on my stomach with my head pillowed on my two hands with my eyes closed under the Christmas tree. Around the base of that tree was a little, cheap train set. Just a simple circle of track with a five-car set-up not counting the steam engine. It has a little glowing headlight more like the tail of a lightning bug, then the great lamps of my youth. I had closed my eyes. It was the end of the day and here this 56-year-old man lay. There was a distinct clickety-clack of the wheels on the tracks as the little thing went around and around, and though it was very small, it made the slightest tremble in the carpet as it passed where my heart was pressed.

It was late at night, and I was sleepy. I dozed off under there with the train going around and around. I could hear it and feel it all again, and before I realized it big tears were rolling down my face and past my lips, leaving a trail of memories tasting like salt. I was there: the viaduct, the trains, the childhood. This toy weighed ounces compared to the monsters that weighed tons. The little thing was no match for the event, but the memories were. They always are.

The thunder has, of course, long since passed over my head and to a great degree through my life. I've ridden trains all over this country and in Britain and Africa and the Pacific rim. Now I fly, but as the great jet engines whine, they are but a whimper when compared to the blast of steam releasing or the great whistle or the shear thunder of the thing passing over my head. Those wheels slipping on the tracks as the great beast tries to gain purchase on the rails. The sparks flying as steel screamed against steel and movement began — usually backward at first to tighten up the couplings. And then, the forward lunge and the eventual momentum as car after car jerked the one behind it into motion. Soon it was moving.

I could feel it in my heart, and how I longed for a moment in the sun of a long ago, hot Chicago day. To smell the strong stench of the world's greatest stockyards as the wind blew in our direction. And the refuge of my fort, my castle, my childhood existential home, my viaduct.

A 56-year-old man not really crying, just lubricating memories. And why not? It's the continuity of our lives. It's the end to end that counts. It's the whole unit. It's what literary people call "story."

With my head under a Christmas tree as the embers burned to a glow in the fireplace warming my back against a cold, wet Kansas night, I was there where I belonged. And I wept a silent heart-ache for so much. And all of it was a mixture too complex to even attempt to relate. Rattle, rattle, rattle, it would go by, and with my eyes closed I was there. I reached out my hand for a little red dump truck, but it was gone, of course, with the years. So be it. It should be gone. My little red dump truck hauled off somewhere. It's in a junk store window or smashed flat and all but a wisp of rust in a Chicago dump. I don't like that, but such is life. Ashes to ashes, dust to dust. And so shall it be with me. And so it should be.

But for now, I'll close my eyes in the quiet great room of my home as the others I love and the memories I remember sleep, and I'll be there again. My little toy train. It may be the greatest Christmas present I've ever received and, oh yes, I really could feel it in my heart.